THE KINGDOM ACCORDING TO JESUS

A Study of Jesus' Parables on the Kingdom of Heaven

Rob Phillips

CrossBooks
1663 Liberty Drive
Bloomington, IN 47403
www.crossbooks.com

© 2009 Rob Phillips. All rights reserved.

No part of this book may be reproduced, stored in a retrieval system, or transmitted by any means without the written permission of the author.

First published by CrossBooks 5/28/2009

ISBN: 978-1-6150-7025-1 (sc)

Printed in the United States of America
Bloomington, Indiana

This book is printed on acid-free paper.

For Dad, whose unflinching faithfulness to the Lord compels me to "seek first the kingdom" (Matt. 6:33).

Contents

Chapter	Title	Scriptures	Page
1	Defining the Kingdom of Heaven		1
2	Why Jesus Used Parables to Describe the Kingdom of Heaven	Matt. 13:10–17, 34-35	7
3	Receiving the Kingdom: *The Parable of the Sower*	Matt. 13:1–9, 18–23	13
4	Kingdoms in Conflict: *The Parable of the Wheat and Tares*	Matt. 13:24–30, 36–43	19
5	The Victorious Underdog: *The Parable of the Mustard Seed and the Parable of the Leaven*	Matt. 13:31–32 Matt. 13:33	25
6	Priceless Value: *The Parable of the Hidden Treasure and the Parable of the Pearl of Great Price*	Matt. 13:44 Matt. 13:45–46	31
7	Cast Out of the Kingdom: *The Parable of the Dragnet (Good and Bad Fish)*	Matt. 13:47–50	37
8	Treasures Old and New: *The Parable of the Storeroom*	Matt. 13:51–53	41
9	The Greatest in the Kingdom: *The Parable of the Child*	Matt. 18:1–9	47
10	The King's Mercy: *The Parable of the Unmerciful Servant*	Matt. 18:21–35	53
11	The Servant's Charge: *The Parable of the Vineyard Laborers*	Matt. 20:1–16	59
12	A Change of Ownership: *The Parable of the Vineyard Owner*	Matt. 21:33–46	65
13	The King's Righteous Anger: *The Parable of the Wedding Banquet*	Matt. 22:1–14	71
14	The King's Delayed Return: *The Parable of the Ten Virgins*	Matt. 25:1–13	77

15	The Separation of the Righteous from the Wicked: *The Parable of the Sheep and Goats*	Matt. 25:31–46	83
16	The Lord of the Harvest: *The Parable of the Growing Seed*	Mark 4:26–29	89
17	The Call to Accountability: *The Parable of the Ten Minas*	Luke 19:11–27	93
Appendix			99

CHAPTER 1
Defining the Kingdom of Heaven

The terms *kingdom of God, kingdom of heaven,* and *kingdom* (with reference to the kingdom of God/heaven) appear nearly 150 times in Scripture. None of these references gives a simple, straightforward definition of the kingdom, and many passages appear to be contradictory. Yet the kingdom is the primary focus of Jesus' teaching. Many of his parables describe the kingdom. The apostles preach the "gospel of the kingdom." And end-times prophecy points us toward the day when God's kingdom will come in its fullness.

So, what is the kingdom of heaven? Are the kingdom of heaven and the kingdom of God the same thing? Is the kingdom here already, or are we to wait for it? What does it look like? Who's in the kingdom and who's not? And what is required to enter the kingdom? We will explore these and other questions in this book, mostly through the lens of Jesus' parables in Matthew on the kingdom of heaven. To begin, we need to understand what the Bible says the kingdom of heaven is—and is not.

What the kingdom of heaven is not

There are many incorrect views about the kingdom that have emerged over the years—among them, that the kingdom of heaven is:

- An inward power, a purely subjective realm of God's power and influence in our lives

- An apocalyptic realm, altogether future and supernatural, that God will install at the end of human history and is by no means present or spiritual

- The church, either the ever-expanding church as the world is Christianized, ushering in the kingdom, or the true church hidden within professing Christianity

- The universe, all of God's creation over which he is sovereign

- Heaven, in contrast to earth

As we'll see, none of these views holds up under a careful study of Scripture.

So ... what is the kingdom of heaven?

The kingdom of heaven simply is God's reign, his authority to rule. The following truths help us understand the kingdom in more practical terms:

- The kingdom is God's conquest, through Jesus Christ, of his enemies: sin, Satan, and death.

- The kingdom comes in stages. It was foretold by Jewish prophets as an everlasting, mighty, and righteous reign involving the nation of Israel and its coming King, the Messiah. It came humbly through the virgin birth of the Son of God and exists today as a "mystery" in the hearts of all believers. In the second coming, the kingdom will at last appear in power and glory. And after Christ's millennial reign on earth, he will deliver the kingdom to the Father, having finally put away sin (it no longer is a reality to be dealt with), Satan (he will be cast into hell to be tormented night and day forever), and death (there is no longer physical or spiritual death).

- The Bible describes this threefold fact: 1) some passages refer to the kingdom as God's reign, rule, or authority; 2) some passages refer to the kingdom as the realm into which we may now enter to experience the blessings of his reign; and 3) some passages refer to the kingdom as a future realm that will come only with the return of Jesus. All three are true (see "Kingdom Chart," page 107).

- As all kingdoms must have a king, Jesus is King of the kingdom of heaven. As King of Kings and Lord of Lords, Jesus is the eternal Son of God to whom, one day, "every knee should bow … and every tongue should confess …" (Phil. 2:10–11).

- People enter the kingdom and become its citizens by faith in Jesus Christ.

The paradox of the kingdom

When we turn to the Scriptures, we find a perplexing diversity of statements about the kingdom, many of them focusing on the now-versus-future aspects of the kingdom of heaven:

- The kingdom is a present spiritual reality (Rom. 14:17); at the same time, it is a future inheritance that God will give his people when Christ returns in glory (Matt. 25:34).

- The kingdom is a realm into which Christians have already entered (Col. 1:13); then again, it is a future realm we will enter when Christ returns (Matt. 8:11; 2 Peter 1:11).

- The kingdom will be ushered in with great glory (Matt. 13:41–43, 24:30); yet, its coming is without signs (Luke 17:20–21).

- The kingdom is present and at work in the world (Luke 13:18–21); still, Jesus tells Pilate, "My kingdom is not of this world" (John 18:36).

- The kingdom is a present reality (Matt. 12:28) and a future blessing (1 Cor. 15:50–57).

- The kingdom is an inner spiritual redemptive blessing (Rom. 14:17) that can only be experienced through the new birth (John 3:3); yet, it will involve world government (Rev. 11:15).

- People enter the kingdom now (Matt. 21:31) and in the future (Matt. 8:11).

- The kingdom is a gift God will give the redeemed in the future (Luke 22:29–30), and yet it must be received in the present (Mark 10:15).

How do we reconcile these seemingly contradictory teachings? Simply by setting aside our modern notion of a kingdom as a physical boundary over which a king rules. "The primary meaning of both the Hebrew word *malkuth* in the Old Testament and of the Greek word *basileia* in the New Testament is the rank, authority and sovereignty exercised by a king. A *basileia* may indeed be a realm over which a sovereign exercises authority; and it may be the people who belong to that realm and over whom authority is exercised; but these are secondary and derived meanings. First of all, a kingdom is the authority to rule, the sovereignty of the king."[1]

Certainly God's kingdom has a realm—the believer's heart today, the earth throughout the millennium, and the restored heavens and earth after sin, Satan, and death are finally put away. However, our understanding of the kingdom will advance more quickly if we remember that the kingdom first and foremost is God's authority to rule.

The kingdom of heaven versus the kingdom of God

The terms *kingdom of heaven* and *kingdom of God* are interchangeable. Only Matthew uses the term *kingdom of heaven*, possibly because his gospel is written to Jews who, for fear of taking God's name in vain, used the word *heaven* when referring to God. Even more likely, Jews would be familiar with the phrase *kingdom of heaven* or *kingdom of the heavens*, while most Greeks would not. Therefore, Mark, Luke, and even Matthew on occasion (Matt. 19:23–24, for example) prefer the term *kingdom of God* to make the text more understandable to Greek readers.

---

[1] *The Gospel of the Kingdom: Scriptural Studies in the Kingdom of God* by George Eldon Ladd, p. 19.

Some commentators believe there *is* a distinction between the kingdom of heaven and the kingdom of God. They say the kingdom of heaven refers to professing Christianity throughout the church age (Pentecost to the rapture), while the kingdom of God spans across time and eternity. But this view does not hold up since some of Jesus' parables about the kingdom of heaven in Matthew are recorded in other gospels as relating to the kingdom of God. We should not try to force a separate meaning on the kingdom of heaven just because Matthew preferred that term.

The "world" versus the "age"

Two Greek words are translated as "world" in older translations of Scripture: *kosmos* and *aion*. They are not the same, and translating both words as "world" obscures what God's Word says about his kingdom.

Kosmos refers to something in proper order or harmony. In its most common usage in Scripture, *kosmos* is the created universe. In contrast, *aion* designates a period of time and ought to be translated "age." Matthew 12:32 is a good example of *aion* being translated to "world" in the King James Version, when it should be translated to "age": "Whoever speaks a word against the Son of Man, it will be forgiven him. But whoever speaks against the Holy Spirit, it will not be forgiven him, either in this age or in the one to come" (HCSB).

When *kosmos* and *aion* are properly translated, we begin to see that God's Word tells us about two ages: This Age (from the fall to the second coming of Christ), followed by The Age to Come. This Age is dominated by sin (Gal. 1:4), while The Age to Come will be characterized by righteousness. For a graphic depiction of this teaching, see page 105.

The mystery of the kingdom

Finally, it's important to understand that many of Jesus' parables deal with the "mystery" of the kingdom of heaven (Matt. 13:11). The Greek word for mystery, or secret, is *mysteria* and means what we can know only by divine revelation. This has particular value in helping us understand the kingdom of heaven in this present age. The Jews were looking for a political and military kingdom based on their understanding of the

Old Testament; they completely bypassed the prophecies in Isaiah 53 and elsewhere about the Suffering Servant and thereby rejected Jesus as Messiah.

And so the kingdom of heaven is here in the person of Jesus. But the mystery of the kingdom is that it must first come without fanfare in the Lamb of God who, through his death, burial, and resurrection, would take away the sin of the world. The kingdom will come in power and great glory one day when Jesus returns as the Lion of the Tribe of Judah (see Rev. 19:11–16).

CHAPTER 2

Why Jesus Used Parables to Describe the Kingdom of Heaven

Matthew 13:10–17, 34–35 (HCSB)

¹⁰ Then the disciples came up and asked Him, "Why do You speak to them in parables?"

¹¹ He answered them, "Because the secrets of the kingdom of heaven have been given for you to know, but it has not been given to them.

¹² For whoever has, [more] will be given to him, and he will have more than enough. But whoever does not have, even what he has will be taken away from him.

¹³ For this reason I speak to them in parables, because looking they do not see, and hearing they do not listen or understand.

¹⁴ Isaiah's prophecy is fulfilled in them, which says: **You will listen and listen, yet never understand; and you will look and look, yet never perceive.**

¹⁵ **For this people's heart has grown callous; their ears are hard of hearing, and they have shut their eyes; otherwise they might see with their eyes and hear with their ears, understand with their hearts and turn back— and I would cure them.**

¹⁶ But your eyes are blessed because they do see, and your ears because they do hear!

¹⁷ For I assure you: Many prophets and righteous people longed to see the things you see yet didn't see them; to hear the things you hear yet didn't hear them."

³⁴ Jesus told the crowds all these things in parables, and He would not speak anything to them without a parable,

³⁵ so that what was spoken through the prophet might be fulfilled: **I will open My mouth in parables; I will declare things kept secret from the foundation of the world.**

What is a parable?

A parable is a story drawn from everyday experience to illustrate a deeper truth—in Scripture, a spiritual truth. The teaching of parables goes back to antiquity. The first parable recorded in the Bible is that of the trees choosing for themselves a king (Judges 9:7–15). There are numerous parables in both the Old and New Testaments, but the most common parables are those taught by Jesus. While Jesus was not the first to use parables, he endowed them with unparalleled originality and spiritual depth. In fact, more than one-third of all his recorded sayings are parables.

Two Greek words are translated "parable" in the New Testament: *parabole* (forty-eight times), meaning "to represent or stand for something," and *paroimia* (four times in John), meaning "an adage, dark saying, proverb, a presentation deviating from the usual means of speaking." As Herbert Lockyer writes in *All the Parables of the Bible,* "Parables prove that the external is the mirror in which we may behold the internal and the spiritual." Parables also reward the faithful learner. As Matthew Henry writes in his unabridged commentary, "A parable is a shell that keeps good fruit for the diligent, but keeps it from the slothful."

Parables and the mystery of the kingdom

Many of Jesus' parables describe the mystery, or secret, of the kingdom of God (Mark 4:11). The term "mystery" refers to something God has held in secret throughout the ages but has finally disclosed in a new revelation of his redemptive work. In this case, the mystery of the kingdom is that God's kingdom has come in an unexpected way—a way not fully revealed in the Old Testament.

With the coming of Jesus the Messiah as the Lamb of God, or the Suffering Servant, he invades Satan's kingdom and reigns in the hearts of men. Yes, the day will come when God's kingdom overcomes human authority, when the Lion of Judah appears in power and great glory to sit on the throne of David and rule the earth, but first he must come humbly and lay down his life as a ransom for lost sinners, destroying the enemies of God: sin, Satan, and death. Jesus uses parables to reveal these previously hidden truths about the kingdom.

George Eldon Ladd puts it this way in *The Gospel of the Kingdom:* "But the mystery, the new revelation, is that this very Kingdom of God has now come to work among men but in an utterly unexpected way. It is not now destroying human rule; it is not now abolishing sin from the earth; it is not now bringing the baptism of fire that John had announced. It has come quietly, unobtrusively, secretly. It can work among men and never be recognized by the crowds. In the spiritual realm, the Kingdom now offers to men the blessings of God's rule, delivering them from the power of Satan and sin. The Kingdom of God is an offer, a gift which may be accepted or rejected. The Kingdom is now here with persuasion rather than with power."[2]

Why Jesus used parables

In Matthew 13, after Jesus tells the parable of the sower, his disciples ask him why he is now employing this form of teaching. His answer is revealing:

- Because the mysteries or secrets of the kingdom have been given to Jesus' disciples but not to others (v. 11). Jesus would spend three full years with the apostles, teaching them about the necessity of his death, burial, and resurrection. Others would be taught the mystery in parables and, if they inclined their hearts toward God, would understand.

---

2 *The Gospel of the Kingdom: Scriptural Studies in the Kingdom of God* by George Eldon Ladd, p. 55.

- Those who received the gospel of the kingdom would benefit from the truths revealed in Jesus' parables, while those who insisted on a political and military Messiah would no longer be entrusted with the Scriptures—a reference to the Jewish religious leaders (v. 12).

- Those who already reject Jesus as Messiah are so hard of heart they cannot understand these simple parables. Just as the Jews in Isaiah's days had rejected God—leading to judgment—so the unbelieving Jews of Jesus' day would face judgment in the destruction of the temple in 70 AD, as well as judgment after the kingdom comes in power (vv. 13–15). As Matthew Henry has written, "A parable, like the pillar of cloud and fire, turns a dark side towards Egyptians, which confounds them, but a light side towards the Israelites, which comforts them, and so answers a double intention."

- Jesus' parables of the kingdom reveal spiritual truths that the prophets of old could only see in shadow form; the apostles should rejoice that they are witnessing the coming of the kingdom in mystery (vv. 16–17).

- Jesus' parables fulfill prophecy. The psalmist wrote that Messiah would "declare wise sayings; I will speak mysteries from the past" (Ps. 78:2), and that's exactly what Jesus did (v. 35). See also Deut. 29:29; Rom. 16:25; 1 Cor. 2:7; Eph. 3:9; and Col. 1:26.

How we should study Jesus' parables of the kingdom

We will study Jesus' parables of the kingdom by considering:

1. **Context.** We will ask: To whom is Jesus speaking? When? Where? Why? Who else is present? How does this parable compare with other parables and teachings of Jesus, and with other Scriptures?

2. **Theme.** We will locate the central theme. Parables normally focus on a single key point. Jesus' parables of the kingdom reveal key aspects of his reign.
3. **Character(s).** We will identify the central character or characters and see how each relates to the central theme. We'll also ask what role the other characters play in the parable.
4. **Details.** We will look at the details of each parable, being careful not to impose unintended meanings.
5. **Personal Application.** We will explore what understanding, attitude, or action Jesus is demanding of his listeners—and of us.

The design of speaking in parables

According to *Barnes' Notes on the New Testament,* Jesus has the following four things in mind as he tells each parable:

1. To convey truth in a more interesting manner to the mind. Adding to the truth conveyed the beauty of a lovely image or narrative.

2. To teach spiritual truth so as to arrest the attention of ignorant people. This makes an appeal to them through the *senses.*

3. To convey some offensive truth, some pointed personal rebuke, in such a way as to bring it *home* to the conscience. Of this kind was the parable that Nathan delivered to David (2 Sam. 12:1–7) and many of our Savior's parables addressed to the Jews.

4. To *conceal* from one part of his audience truths which he intended others should understand. Thus Christ often, by this means, delivered truths to his disciples in the presence of the Jews, which he well knew the Jews would not understand—truths pertaining to them particularly, and which he was under no obligation to explain to the Jews (see Matt. 13:13–16; Mark 4:33).

Chapter 3

Receiving the Kingdom: The Parable of the Sower

Matthew 13:1–9, 18–23 (HCSB)

¹ On that day Jesus went out of the house and was sitting by the sea.

² Such large crowds gathered around Him that He got into a boat and sat down, while the whole crowd stood on the shore.

³ Then He told them many things in parables, saying: "Consider the sower who went out to sow.

⁴ As he was sowing, some seeds fell along the path, and the birds came and ate them up.

⁵ Others fell on rocky ground, where there wasn't much soil, and they sprang up quickly since the soil wasn't deep.

⁶ But when the sun came up they were scorched, and since they had no root, they withered.

⁷ Others fell among thorns, and the thorns came up and choked them.

⁸ Still others fell on good ground, and produced a crop: some 100, some 60, and some 30 times [what was sown].

⁹ Anyone who has ears should listen!"

18 "You, then, listen to the parable of the sower:

19 When anyone hears the word about the kingdom and doesn't understand it, the evil one comes and snatches away what was sown in his heart. This is the one sown along the path.

20 And the one sown on rocky ground—this is one who hears the word and immediately receives it with joy.

21 Yet he has no root in himself, but is short-lived. When pressure or persecution comes because of the word, immediately he stumbles.

22 Now the one sown among the thorns—this is one who hears the word, but the worries of this age and the seduction of wealth choke the word, and it becomes unfruitful.

23 But the one sown on the good ground—this is one who hears and understands the word, who does bear fruit and yields: some 100, some 60, some 30 times [what was sown]."

This parable also is found in Mark 4:1–9, 13–20 and in Luke 8:4–8, 11–15.

The context

Jesus probably is staying with Peter at his home in Capernaum. He has just tussled with the scribes and Pharisees who accused him of eating "unlawfully" and of healing on the Sabbath. He has foiled a plot by the Pharisees to kill him. He has cast a demon out of a man and then answered the Pharisees' accusation that he is casting out demons by Satan's power. He has rebuked the Pharisees for demanding a sign that he is the Christ. And he has denied his own family's request to see him by declaring that his family consists of all who believe in him. Now, in chapter 13, the Scripture says in verse 1, "On that day Jesus went out of the house and was sitting by the sea [of Galilee]."

It is significant that in chapter 12 Jesus shows clear evidence that he is the Messiah and that his kingdom has invaded Satan's kingdom:

- He declares himself greater than the temple and is indeed "Lord of the Sabbath."

- He casts out demons and heals the sick.

- He foretells his death, burial, and resurrection as the one sure sign that he is the Son of God.

- He rebukes the Jews of his generation for their wickedness and foretells their judgment (which falls in 70 AD).

- He declares that his true family is not earthly but heavenly, not of flesh and blood but of spirit.

Matthew 12:28 is crucial in setting the stage for Jesus' parables in chapter 13: "If I drive out demons by the Spirit of God, then the kingdom of God has come to you." Jesus declares that the long-awaited kingdom of heaven has come—but not in the way the Jewish leaders were expecting. Rather than as a political and military machine, the kingdom has come quietly and with great spiritual power, invading Satan's kingdom and binding him (the "strong man" of Matthew 12:29) so that Christ may plunder the evil one's kingdom (see "Present Reality, Future Hope," page 106).

The scribes and Pharisees will have none of this teaching, instead rejecting the King and his kingdom. So in Matthew chapter 13, as Jesus leaves Peter's house and sits beside the sea, multitudes gather around him, having witnessed his miracles and having heard his declaration that the kingdom of heaven has come. So Jesus gets into a boat—perhaps Peter's boat or a boat made available for Jesus' use whenever he needed it—and begins a series of eight parables on the kingdom of heaven. In this first parable— the parable of the sower—it is possible that farmers on the hillsides along the sea were in their fields sowing seed, with the ever-present birds hovering in the air above them.

Central theme

The central theme of this parable is that the kingdom of heaven has come among men and yet men can reject it. As George Eldon Ladd writes, "The mystery of the Kingdom is this: The Kingdom of God is here but not with irresistible power. The Kingdom of God has come, but it is not like a stone grinding an image to powder. It is not now destroying wickedness. On the contrary, it is like a man sowing seed.

It does not force itself upon men … This was a staggering thing to one who knew only the Old Testament … One day God will indeed manifest His mighty power to purge the earth of wickedness, sin and evil; but not now. God's Kingdom is working among men, but God will not compel them to bow before it. They must receive it; the response must come from a willing heart and a submissive will."[3]

Central character

Christ no doubt is the sower, but in a sense every believer who shares the gospel is a sower as well. In Jesus' day, farmers walked through their fields scattering seed by hand broadly across their property, knowing that a high percentage of the seed would not bear fruit. Normally, another member of the family would follow the sower closely and plow the seed under. But many of the seeds were eaten by birds as they fell on footpaths; others landed in shallow soil with a stratum of rock beneath; and still other seeds fell at the fringes of the property among thornbushes that the farmers used to build small cooking fires. Still, the seed is broadcast widely, and some seed finds the good soil, thus raising up a crop.

Details

Jesus interprets the parable for his disciples:

- The seed is the word of God (Luke 8:11)—the good news that the kingdom has come in the person of Jesus the Messiah, and that all may enter into the kingdom by faith in him, the Word (*Logos*, John 1:1).

- The birds represent Satan, who "takes away the word from their hearts, so that they may not believe and be saved" (Luke 8:12).

- The seed along the path stands for the impact of the word on hearers who do not understand. Their hearts are hardened like the footpaths winding through ancient wheat fields. They cannot believe because they will not believe, much like the Jewish leaders Jesus described in Matthew 13:12–15.

---

3   *The Gospel of the Kingdom*, pp. 56–57.

- The seed on the rocky ground represents the impact of the word on shallow, uncommitted hearers. They may have an emotional response to the gospel but walk away when the reality of kingdom living—which may include pressure or persecution—sets in. Jesus' followers who left him in John 6:66 are examples of those who loved Jesus' miracles but balked at the call to discipleship.

- The seed among the thorns illustrates the impact of the word on worldly hearers. Though they understand the gospel of the kingdom, they prefer the "worries, riches, and pleasures of life" (Luke 8:14). The rich young ruler who encountered Jesus falls into this category of hearers (Luke 18:18–23).

- The seed in the good ground represents the impact of the word on those who, "having heard the word with an honest and good heart, hold on to it and by enduring, bear fruit" (Luke 8:15)—"some 100, some 60, some 30 times [what was sown]" (Matt. 13:23).

Spiritual application

In Jesus' day, farmers sowed widely across their fields, knowing that perhaps one in three seeds would grow to maturity. As believers, we are to sow the gospel of the kingdom widely and indiscriminately, trusting God to grant the harvest.

Regarding the kingdom, Jesus' parable of the sower is a clear message that his kingdom would not at this time come in power and great glory; instead, it would reside in the hearts of willing believers and be resisted by many. This is not what the Jews were expecting, and many rejected Jesus and his call to the kingdom because he is not the political and military leader they sought. At the same time, Satan, whose kingdom Jesus has invaded, will hover watchfully and snatch the gospel away from those whose hearts are hardened against it, lest, person by person, he lose power as "the god of this age" (2 Cor. 4:4). [See a graphic depiction of this parable on page 102.]

CHAPTER 4

Kingdoms in Conflict: The Parable of the Wheat and Tares

Matthew 13:24–30, 36–43 (HCSB)

[24] He presented another parable to them: "The kingdom of heaven may be compared to a man who sowed good seed in his field.

[25] But while people were sleeping, his enemy came, sowed weeds among the wheat, and left.

[26] When the plants sprouted and produced grain, then the weeds also appeared.

[27] The landowner's slaves came to him and said, 'Master, didn't you sow good seed in your field? Then where did the weeds come from?'

[28] "'An enemy did this!' he told them. "'So, do you want us to go and gather them up?' the slaves asked him.

[29] "'No,' he said. 'When you gather up the weeds, you might also uproot the wheat with them.

[30] Let both grow together until the harvest. At harvest time I'll tell the reapers: Gather the weeds first and tie them in bundles to burn them, but store the wheat in my barn.'"

³⁶ Then He dismissed the crowds and went into the house. His disciples approached Him and said, "Explain the parable of the weeds in the field to us."

³⁷ He replied: "The One who sows the good seed is the Son of Man;

³⁸ the field is the world; and the good seed—these are the sons of the kingdom. The weeds are the sons of the evil one, and

³⁹ the enemy who sowed them is the Devil. The harvest is the end of the age, and the harvesters are angels.

⁴⁰ Therefore just as the weeds are gathered and burned in the fire, so it will be at the end of the age.

⁴¹ The Son of Man will send out His angels, and they will gather from His kingdom everything that causes sin and those guilty of lawlessness.

⁴² They will throw them into the blazing furnace where there will be weeping and gnashing of teeth.

⁴³ Then the righteous will shine like the sun in their Father's kingdom. Anyone who has ears should listen!"

The context

Jesus continues teaching the crowds from his boat at the shoreline of the Sea of Galilee. He has just explained the parable of the sower to his disciples, as well as why he is teaching the mysteries of the kingdom in parables (see chapters 2 and 3). Now, without further delay, Matthew records that Jesus "presented another parable to them" (v. 24). As with the parable of the sower, Jesus later explains the parable of the wheat and tares to his disciples.

Keep in mind what Jesus has said in Matthew 12:28. It is crucial in setting the stage for Jesus' parables in chapter 13: "If I drive out demons by the Spirit of God, then the kingdom of God has come to you." Jesus declares that the long-awaited kingdom of heaven has come, but not in the way the Jewish leaders were expecting. Rather than as a political and military machine, the kingdom has come quietly and with great spiritual power, invading Satan's kingdom and binding him (the "strong man" of Matthew 12:29) so that he may plunder the evil one's kingdom.

Once again, the scribes and Pharisees will have none of this teaching and reject the King and his kingdom. So in chapter 13, as Jesus leaves Peter's house and sits beside the sea, multitudes gather around him, having witnessed his miracles and having heard his declaration that the kingdom of heaven has come. Jesus gets into a boat and begins a series of eight parables on the kingdom of heaven. The parable of the wheat and tares is the second of these parables.

Central theme

The central theme of this parable is that God's kingdom and Satan's kingdom will exist side-by-side during this "present evil age" (Gal. 1:4). Contrary to the Jewish expectation that the Messiah would be a conquering political king, Jesus comes the first time as the Suffering Servant to invade Satan's kingdom and rescue his own out of it (Col. 1:13). This is the "mystery" of the kingdom. The day will come when Jesus "abolishes all rule and all authority and power" (1 Cor. 15:24), but that day takes place in the future. For now, believers and unbelievers will live together—in many cases indistinguishable from one another—until the resurrection and judgment.

Central characters

The "good seed" are believers and the "weeds" or "tares" are unbelievers—more specifically, unbelievers who are "holding to the form of religion but denying its power" (2 Tim. 3:5). *Manners and Customs of Bible Lands* by Fred Wight gives us a clearer image of these false professors of the faith by describing the nature of tares:

In the Holy Land, tares are something called 'wild wheat,' because they resemble wheat, only the grains are black. Thomson has this to say about the tares:

> The Arabic name for tares is *zawan*, and they abound all over the East, and are a great nuisance to the farmer. The grain is small, and is arranged along the upper part of the stalk,

> which stands perfectly erect. Its taste is bitter, and when eaten separately, or when diffused in ordinary bread, it causes dizziness, and often acts as an emetic. In short, it is a strong soporific poison, and must be carefully winnowed, and picked out of the wheat, grain by grain, before grinding, or the flour is not healthy. Of course the farmers are very anxious to exterminate it, but that is nearly impossible.

Interestingly, Satan's deception is so great that even the tares suppose themselves to be children of the kingdom (Matt. 7:21–23).

Details

Jesus describes himself (the Son of Man) as the sower. Apart from him, there is no everlasting life. And like the sower in his preceding parable (Matt. 13:1–9), Jesus determined that the gospel of the kingdom would be spread broadly, taking root across all racial and ethnic lines (Rev. 5:9–10). That's why the "good seed," or believers, would not just be restricted to the nation of Israel.

"The field" is the world, the mass of humanity stretched across the globe. God has placed believers everywhere.

"The enemy" is Satan, who craftily plants his counterfeit Christians wherever believers spring up. He does so "while people are sleeping," a warning to the church to be ever vigilant against false teachers who, Paul says, are "savage wolves" bent on destroying the flock (Acts 20:29–31).

"The harvest" is the end of the age—this present evil age as mentioned in Galatians 1:4—at which time God will separate true believers from false ones.

"The harvesters" are God's angels, who assist him in resurrection and judgment (Matt. 24:30–31).

Spiritual application

The day is coming, says Jesus, when there will be a harvest and a gathering. This refers to the resurrection and judgment in which he will separate believers from nonbelievers (John 5:28–29). Just as the tares are gathered and burned, those who have rejected Christ will receive the same judgment pronounced on Satan: everlasting separation from God in hell (Matt. 25:41; Rev. 20:10–15).

Believers, however, will receive glorified bodies similar to Christ's resurrected body. They will be rewarded for their faithfulness and spend eternity with their Savior (John 14:1–3; Rom. 14:10; 1 Cor. 3:11–15; 1 Cor. 15:51–57; 1 Thess. 4:13–17; Rev. 21:1–8).

While eagerly anticipating that day, believers should be diligent to "confirm your calling and election" (2 Peter 1:10) and to be on guard against false professors of the faith who are wolves in sheep's clothing (Matt. 7:15).

CHAPTER 5

The Victorious Underdog: The Parable of the Mustard Seed and the Parable of the Leaven

Matthew 13:31–33 (HCSB)

[31] He presented another parable to them: "The kingdom of heaven is like a mustard seed that a man took and sowed in his field.

[32] It's the smallest of all the seeds, but when grown, it's taller than the vegetables and becomes a tree, so that the birds of the sky come and nest in its branches."

[33] He told them another parable: "The kingdom of heaven is like yeast that a woman took and mixed into 50 pounds of flour until it spread through all of it."

The parable of the mustard seed also is found in Mark 4:30–32 and in Luke 13:18–19.

The parable of the leaven also is found in Luke 13:20–21.

The context

Jesus continues teaching the crowds from a boat at the shoreline of the Sea of Galilee. Already, he has given them the parable of the sower and the parable of the wheat and tares. He has explained to his disciples the meaning of the parable of the sower, as well as why he is teaching the mysteries of the kingdom in parables. Later, he will explain the meaning of the parable of the wheat and tares. For now, he presents two short parables that describe how the kingdom of heaven begins humbly, almost imperceptibly, on earth.

Remember what Jesus said in Matthew 12:28; it is crucial in understanding his parables in chapter 13: "If I drive out demons by the Spirit of God, then the kingdom of God has come to you." Jesus declares that the long-awaited kingdom of heaven has come—but not in the way the Jewish leaders were expecting. Rather than as a political and military machine, the kingdom has come quietly and with great spiritual power, invading Satan's kingdom and binding him (the "strong man" of Matthew 12:29) so that he may plunder the evil one's kingdom.

Once again, the scribes and Pharisees will have none of this teaching and reject the King and his kingdom. So in chapter 13, Jesus leaves Peter's house and sits beside the sea. Multitudes gather around him, having witnessed his miracles and having heard his declaration that the kingdom of heaven has come. Jesus gets into a boat and begins a series of eight parables on the kingdom of heaven. The parables of the mustard seed and leaven are the third and fourth of these parables.

The Mustard Seed

Central theme

The central theme of this parable is that the kingdom of heaven has begun on earth humbly, almost imperceptibly. It is compared to a tiny, insignificant mustard seed; in fact, to ancient Jews the mustard seed was the proverbial symbol of something of little importance. Nevertheless, it is God's kingdom and must not be despised or ignored.

It should be noted that some see this parable as an illustration of the monumental growth of the kingdom, from humble beginnings to towering majesty. True, the kingdom starts small, then grows quickly and powerfully. From 120 believers gathered to pray following Jesus' ascension, the early church grows to more than 3,000 in a single day following Peter's sermon on the day of Pentecost (see Acts. 1:15 and 2:41). Yet this is not the key point of the parable, for Jesus could have used better illustrations, like an oak, to illustrate a sturdy and towering kingdom. His point is to emphasize the "mystery" that the kingdom, as a present reality, is not in the form Jewish leaders are expecting.

George Ladd comments: "The Kingdom of God … is here as something tiny, as something insignificant, as something as small as a mustard seed. The important thing is that even though it is like a tiny seed, it is still the Kingdom of God. Jesus says, 'Do not let its apparent insignificance deceive you. Do not be discouraged. The time will come when this same Kingdom of God, which is here like the tiny seed, will be a great shrub, so great that the birds of the heaven will come and lodge in its branches.'"[4]

Central character

The mustard seed, or *khardah*, symbolizes humble beginnings and denotes the smallest of weights and measures.

Details

The great shrub growing from the mustard seed often reaches heights of ten to twenty feet within a matter of months. Some say the "birds" symbolize Satan and his evil ones, who find their place in the church. Others say the birds foretell the denominations of Christendom. But more likely, if there is any significance at all, Jesus uses the birds either to describe the inclusion of the Gentiles, or to illustrate the strength and security believers find in the kingdom.

Spiritual application

Nearly 2,000 years after Jesus told this parable, the kingdom of heaven continues to be more like a mustard seed than a towering tree. But

---

[4] *The Gospel of the Kingdom*, pp. 58–59.

believers should look up. Christ reigns today in the hearts of men, and his kingdom is growing. One day it will be impossible to ignore.

The Leaven

Central theme

The central theme of this parable is the same as the theme of the parable of the mustard seed: the kingdom of heaven has begun on earth humbly, almost imperceptibly. For background, note that the Hebrew housewife could not buy a yeast cake at the corner market. She had to take a piece of dough that already was leavened—containing yeast—and mix it in a batch of unleavened dough, where it would do its work without fanfare.

There are two general interpretations of this parable, both of which miss the main point. First, some say the parable illustrates the gradual but complete spread of the kingdom. Certainly, it's true that yeast works its way through the dough until the entire lump is leavened. And it's true that the kingdom of heaven reaches around the world one heart at a time until people from "every tribe and language and people and nation" become its citizens (Rev. 5:9). But the main point of Jesus' parable has to do with the imperceptible nature of the kingdom; it is not now here in power and glory, as the Jewish leaders expected; rather, it hides itself in people's hearts and comes quietly through its King, a Galilean carpenter.

The second interpretation of this parable is that it illustrates the spread of false teachings throughout the kingdom, since leaven in Scripture normally typifies impurity or evil. It is true that Jesus warned his followers about the leaven of the Pharisees (hypocrisy), Sadducees (rationalism), and Herodians (worldliness) [see Matt. 16:6–12; 22:16–21, 23, 29; 23:27–28; Mark 8:15]. However, as with the parable of the mustard seed, Jesus' point is to show his followers that the kingdom already has come, but not in the way they expected. Not as a glorious political and military machine led by a conquering king, but through the transformation of the human heart made possible by a Suffering Servant.

Central character

The kingdom, Jesus said, is like leaven. So leaven, not the dough or the woman who kneads it, is the central character. The kingdom of heaven, as God's reign, is good; therefore, leaven cannot symbolize evil in this context, even though it normally does in other Scripture passages. The leaven in Jesus' day consisted of a piece of fermented dough kept over from the former baking. This preserved lump of dough either was dissolved in water in the kneading trough before the flour was added, or was "hidden" in the flour and kneaded along with it, as in the case of this parable.

The International Standard Bible Encyclopedia helps draw the distinction: "The figurative uses of leaven in the New Testament, no less than with the rabbis, reflect the ancient view of it as 'corrupt and corrupting,' in parts at least, e.g., Mt 16:6 parallel, and especially the proverbial saying twice quoted by Paul, 'A little leaven leaveneth the whole lump' (1Cor 5:6f; Gal 5:9). But as Jesus used it in Mt 13:33, 'The kingdom of heaven is like unto leaven,' it is clearly the hidden, silent, mysterious but all-pervading and transforming action of the leaven in the measures of flour that is the point of the comparison."

Details

This is such a simple parable that we risk clouding the message by treating it as an allegory. It is true that the woman is used figuratively in Scripture three ways: as a kingdom (Babylon, for example), a city (Jerusalem), and the church (both the true church and the apostate church). Some would argue that the woman in this parable symbolizes the apostate church, which hides her false teachings among true teachings and thus permeates the entire body of Christ with "teachings of demons" (1 Tim. 4:1). Others would argue that the dough signifies the church, or the fellowship believers have with God; in this context both are corrupted by false teachings. But assigning these meanings to the woman and the dough misses the point and fails to recognize that a parable has one simple lesson, not many hidden meanings. So it's best for us to consider the details as "window dressing" and focus on the simple message of this parable: that the kingdom of heaven is among us, but not in the way it was anticipated.

Spiritual application

Though the kingdom of heaven is within the hearts of believers today, and its King is not reigning outwardly, Christians should take heart. The King of Kings and Lord of Lords will return one day in power and great glory, just as surely as the yeast will permeate the dough and rise in the oven.

CHAPTER 6

Priceless Value:
The Parable of the Hidden Treasure and the Parable of the Pearl of Great Price

Matthew 13:44–46 (HCSB)

⁴⁴ "The kingdom of heaven is like treasure, buried in a field, that a man found and reburied. Then in his joy he goes and sells everything he has and buys that field.

⁴⁵ Again, the kingdom of heaven is like a merchant in search of fine pearls.

⁴⁶ When he found one priceless pearl, he went and sold everything he had, and bought it."

The context

Jesus has dismissed the crowds by the Sea of Galilee and retreated to Peter's house. There, he explains to his disciples the parable of the wheat and tares, then offers two parables that illustrate the immense value of the kingdom of heaven. Note the flow of the biblical text:

- In Matthew 12, Jesus declares himself the Messiah, predicts his future resurrection, and states emphatically that the kingdom of heaven has come—but not in the way the Jewish leaders were expecting. Rather than as a political and military machine, the kingdom has come quietly and with great spiritual power. The King has invaded Satan's kingdom and bound him (the "strong man" of Matthew 12:29) so that he may plunder the evil one's kingdom.

- The Jewish religious leaders clearly reject Jesus as Messiah since he does not fit their preconceived mold.

- In Matthew 13, Jesus tells eight parables about the kingdom of heaven to help those who trust in him as Messiah better understand this "mystery" of the kingdom. In the parable of the sower, he shows that the kingdom can be resisted. In the parable of the wheat and tares, he explains that during this phase of the kingdom, believers and unbelievers will exist side-by-side, to be separated after his return one day. In the parables of the mustard seed and leaven, he points out that the kingdom begins quietly, almost imperceptibly.

- Now, Jesus teaches two parables that illustrate the immeasurable value of the kingdom.

The Hidden Treasure

Central theme

The central theme of this parable is that the kingdom of heaven is of immense value. Even though the kingdom has come in humble form—largely escaping the notice of secular historians—it is like a treasure with value transcending every other possession.

Notice how Jesus builds his case for the kingdom: The kingdom has come, but not in the way the Jewish leaders expected. It is here, but it can be resisted (parable of the sower). Its citizens will coexist with unbelievers until Messiah returns (parable of the wheat and tares). It begins humbly, almost imperceptibly, yet it is the kingdom of God (parables of the mustard seed and leaven). It should not be underestimated; the kingdom is of immense value (parables of the hidden treasure and pearl of great price).

Central character

The treasure is the focus of this parable. In Jesus' day, it was not uncommon to bury valuables in the ground to keep them from unscrupulous neighbors, thieves, or marauders. This often was done by men before departing for battle or embarking on long journeys. If they returned safely, they could reclaim their buried treasure. But if they died in battle or failed to return home for any reason, the location of the valuables would remain a secret. Because of this, some people in the Holy Land lived as treasure hunters. The Bible features numerous references to the pursuit of hidden treasure (see, for example, Job 3:20–21; Prov. 2:3–5). Even so, the hidden treasure belonged to the person who owned the property, so the one who discovered the treasure would have to purchase the land to become its rightful owner, or be considered a thief.

It is possible, however, that the treasure to which Jesus refers is an underground mine of gold or silver, whose entrance is discovered by accident. Unlike a pot of money, which easily (although illegally) could be carried away, the mine would require excavation and, no doubt, draw considerable attention. So the discoverer "reburies," or hides again, the entrance to the mine, sells all he has, and buys the field. His actions are questionable, if not unethical; Jesus does not condone this unscrupulous man's tactics any more than he approves of the actions of the unjust steward in Luke 16:1–8. The point is that the man who discovers the treasure finds it to be more valuable than all he owns, and he strikes out with great urgency to make the treasure his.

Details

We should be careful not to read too much into this parable. Some, for example, say the treasure is the church, the field is the world, and the man is Christ. By this interpretation, Christ in his foreknowledge saw such value in the church that he sold all he had—he surrendered his heavenly glory and came to earth—for our salvation, and in the process bought the world. But this is not consistent with Jesus' teaching about the kingdom or with the purpose of his parables. Others argue that the gold or silver mine is the kingdom and Christ is the entrance; indeed, Jesus declared himself to be "the door" (John 10:9) and "the way" (John 14:6), and he urges us to enter the kingdom through "the narrow gate" (Matt. 7:13). In this interpretation, the field is the world and the man is anyone God has drawn to himself. While this explanation seems more in line with Christ's teaching about the kingdom, it still may force more meaning than Jesus intended.

Jesus' parables are realistic stories that communicate a single truth; the details are just "window dressing." The simple meaning of this parable is that the kingdom of heaven is of more value than anything we possess, and it is worth all we have.

Spiritual application

Entrance into the kingdom is worth everything we have; nothing is more precious.

The Pearl of Great Price

Central theme

The central theme of this parable is the same as the theme of the hidden treasure: The kingdom of heaven is a treasure with value transcending every other possession.

Central character

The priceless pearl is this parable's main character. Even though Jesus says the kingdom may be likened unto a merchant in search of fine pearls, it is the great value of the kingdom that he has chosen to emphasize. Pearls are precious stones found in the shells of oysters. Their beauty, size, and rarity make them valuable. In John's vision of heaven, one extraordinarily large pearl makes up each of the twelve gates of New Jerusalem (Rev. 21:21), and only the citizens of the kingdom are welcome inside. Such pearls are unfathomable on earth but serve to illustrate the immeasurable value of the kingdom of heaven.

Details

The merchant is experienced and recognizes the rarest of pearls when he comes upon it. Matthew Henry comments: "All the children of men are busy, seeking goodly pearls: one would be rich, another would be honourable, another would be learned; but the most are imposed upon, and take up with counterfeits for pearls ... Jesus Christ is a Pearl of great price, a Jewel of inestimable value, which will make those who have it rich, truly rich, rich toward God; in having him, we have enough to make us happy here and for ever."

George Eldon Ladd adds context to both the parable of the hidden treasure and the pearl of great price: "The Kingdom of heaven is like a treasure whose value transcends every other possession; it is like a pearl whose acquisition merits the loss of all other goods. Now again, the idea that the man *buys* the field or that the merchant *buys* the pearl has nothing to do with the basic truth of the parable. This parable does not tell us that we can buy salvation. Salvation is by faith, the free gift of God; and Matt. 20:1–16 teaches that the Kingdom is a gift and not a reward which can be earned. Yet even though the Kingdom is a gracious gift, it is also costly. It may cost one his earthly possessions (Mark 10:21), or his friends or the affections of his family or even his very life (Luke 14:26). But cost what it may, the Kingdom of God is like a treasure or a costly pearl whose possession merits any cost."[5]

Spiritual application

People should see the immense value in the kingdom of heaven and willingly give up anything that keeps them from becoming its citizens.

---

5   *The Gospel of the Kingdom*, p. 62.

CHAPTER 7

Cast Out of the Kingdom: The Parable of the Dragnet

Matthew 13:47–50 (HCSB)

47 "Again, the kingdom of heaven is like a large net thrown into the sea. It collected every kind [of fish],

48 and when it was full, they dragged it ashore, sat down, and gathered the good [fish] into containers, but threw out the worthless ones.

49 So it will be at the end of the age. The angels will go out, separate the evil people from the righteous,

50 and throw them into the blazing furnace. In that place there will be weeping and gnashing of teeth.

The context

Jesus has dismissed the crowds and gone back into Peter's house. There, he explains to his disciples the parable of the wheat and tares, offers two parables that illustrate the priceless value of the kingdom of heaven, and launches into the parable of the dragnet, also known as the parable of the good and bad fish. Keep in mind how Jesus ties these parables together to deepen his disciples' understanding of the kingdom of heaven:

- The parable of the sower illustrates that the kingdom can be resisted. The Messiah the Jewish leaders are looking for—political and military—will indeed come one day in power and great glory, but first he must come humbly as the Lamb of God. Many will resist, reject, or oppose him.

- The parable of the wheat and tares teaches that throughout this present evil age, believers and unbelievers will live side-by-side, only to be separated and judged one day.

- The parables of the mustard seed and leaven show that the kingdom already has come—but quietly, almost imperceptibly.

- The parables of the hidden treasure and priceless pearl demonstrate that the kingdom is of immeasurable value.

- And now, the parable of the dragnet teaches the blunt truth that those outside the kingdom will be separated eternally from God in hell.

Central theme

The central theme of this parable is that in the age to come, God will separate the citizens of the kingdom of heaven from those in Satan's kingdom. All who reject the King and his kingdom will depart from God and spend eternity in hell. It is a stark teaching, blunt yet simple. And it underscores the fact, taught in the parable of the wheat and tares, that believers and unbelievers will live side-by-side throughout the present evil age, until a day of reckoning comes.

Central character

Jesus says the kingdom is like a dragnet. This is a large net that fishermen used in Jesus' day, weighted on one side with lead and buoyed on the opposite edge by wooden floats or corks. The net often is spread between two fishing boats, enabling cooperating fishermen to capture fish across a wide area from the seabed to the surface of the water. Once the net is cast, either the fishermen in both boats work together to haul

The Kingdom According to Jesus

in the net, or fishermen on the shore, with ropes connected to the net, draw it into the shallow waters. After the catch, the fishermen separate the good fish from the bad.

The dragnet pictures the scope of God's kingdom during this present evil age (Gal. 1:4) and implies the cooperative effort believers engage in to serve Christ in "bringing many sons to glory" (Heb. 2:10). The use of a dragnet, since it catches good and bad fish, requires a time of evaluation and separation. This pictures the resurrection and judgment that will come upon all people at the end of this present age. Jesus speaks of this resurrection and final judgment in John 5:28–29. The New Testament writers indicate an undesignated interval of time between the resurrection of the just ("first resurrection" or "rapture"—1 Cor. 15:51–57; 1 Thess. 4:13–17) and the resurrection of the unjust ("second resurrection" that leads to the "second death" or "the lake of fire"—Rev. 20:11–15). This does not contradict Jesus' parable. Keep in mind that parables are designed to teach a single truth, in this case, the truth of a future resurrection and judgment for all people.

George Eldon Ladd comments:

> "When God brings His Kingdom, the society of wicked men will be displaced by the society of those who have submitted themselves to God's rule who will then enjoy the fullness of the divine blessings freed from all evil. Jesus taught that the redemptive purposes of God had brought His Kingdom to work among men in advance of the Day of Judgment. It is now like a drag-net which gathers within its influence men of various sorts, both good and bad. The separation between the good and the evil is not yet; the Day of Judgment belongs to the end of the age (Matt. 13:49). Meanwhile, there will be within the circle of those who are caught up by the activity of God's Kingdom in the world not only those who are truly sons of the Kingdom; evil men will also be found in this movement."[6]

---

6   *The Gospel of the Kingdom*, pp. 62–63.

Details

The sea is the world, or the mass of fallen humanity (see Isa. 57:20). The fishermen may be seen in two ways: 1) as believers who work cooperatively to spread the gospel; and 2) as angels whom Christ sends out to separate believers from unbelievers (Matt. 13:41, 49; 24:31). The fish are lost people who respond in some way to the gospel of the kingdom. Jesus said some of every kind are taken in, just as John records in Rev. 5:9 that people "from every tribe and language and people and nation" are in heaven. And, of course, the separation of the good and bad fish symbolizes the separation of the just from the unjust in final judgment. Just as some fish caught in the net are cast away, some professors of the faith will be exposed as unbelievers and cast out of the kingdom (see Matt. 7:21–23).

Spiritual application

Peter urges believers to "make every effort to confirm your calling and election" (2 Peter 1:10). At the same time, all professors of Christianity should examine their hearts to see whether they have truly trusted in Christ for their salvation. Are their hearts like good soil (Matt. 13:8)? Is the evidence of their profession like wheat or tares (Matt. 13:24–30)? Finally, all believers, like good fishermen, should cooperate with others to spread the net of the gospel message around the world (Matt. 28:19–20).

CHAPTER 8

Treasures Old and New: The Parable of the Storeroom

Matthew 13:51–53 (HCSB)

⁵¹ "Have you understood all these things?" "Yes," they told Him.

⁵² "Therefore," He said to them, "every student of Scripture instructed in the kingdom of heaven is like a landowner who brings out of his storeroom what is new and what is old."

⁵³ When Jesus had finished these parables, He left there.

The context

Jesus is still in Peter's house, having earlier dismissed the crowds at the shore. He explains to his disciples the parable of the wheat and tares; offers two parables that illustrate the priceless value of the kingdom of heaven; launches into the parable of the dragnet, also known as the parable of the good and bad fish; and finally gives the parable of the storeroom—the last of eight parables of the kingdom in Matthew 13. Keep in mind how Jesus ties these parables together to deepen his disciples' understanding of the "mystery" of the kingdom of heaven:

- The parable of the sower illustrates that the kingdom can be resisted. The Messiah the Jewish leaders are looking for—political and military—will indeed come one day in power and

- The parable of the wheat and tares teaches that throughout this present evil age, believers and unbelievers will live side-by-side, to be separated and judged one day.

- The parables of the mustard seed and leaven show that the kingdom already has come—but quietly, almost imperceptibly.

- The parables of the hidden treasure and priceless pearl demonstrate that the kingdom is of immeasurable value.

- The parable of the dragnet teaches the blunt truth that those outside the kingdom will be separated eternally from God in hell.

- Now, the parable of the storeroom makes it clear that those who understand the kingdom are to share its good news liberally.

Central theme

The central theme of this parable is that the gospel of the kingdom is to be shared liberally. Jesus teaches his disciples the "mystery" of the kingdom—a more complete understanding of the Old Testament prophecies about the kingdom of heaven and their fulfillment in the person of Jesus of Nazareth. In turn, they are to take these "old" and "new" treasures and teach them to others.

The *Life Application Bible* comments:

> Anyone who understands God's real purpose in the law as revealed in the Old Testament has a real treasure. The Old Testament points the way to Jesus, the Messiah. Jesus always upheld its authority and relevance. But there is a double benefit to those who understand Jesus' teaching about the kingdom of heaven. This was a new treasure that Jesus was revealing. Both the old and new teaching give practical guidelines for

faith and for living in the world. The religious leaders, however, were trapped in the old and blind to the new. They were looking for a future kingdom *preceded* by judgment. Jesus, however, taught that the kingdom was *now* and the judgment was future. The religious leaders were looking for a physical and temporal kingdom (via military rebellion and physical rule), but they were blind to the spiritual significance of the kingdom that Christ brought.

Adam Clarke sheds even more light on this theme in his *Commentary*: "No man can properly understand the Old Testament but through the medium of the New, nor can the New be so forcibly or successfully applied to the conscience of a sinner as through the medium of the Old. The law is still a schoolmaster to lead men to Christ—by it is the knowledge of sin, and, without it, there can be no conviction—where it ends, the Gospel begins, as by the Gospel alone is salvation from sin."

Central character

The landowner is the central character in this parable. Experienced and wise, he has stored up an abundance from previous harvests to complement the fresh meat, fruits and vegetables his land now produces, and he makes these available to all entrusted to his care. Even more, the other things he owns are secure and dedicated for sharing with those who come under his roof. Jesus says, "Every student of Scripture instructed in the kingdom of heaven" is like this landowner, taking the riches of the Old Testament and adding to them Christ's teaching on the "mystery" of the kingdom, thus "correctly teaching the word of truth" (2 Tim. 2:15).

Adam Clarke further comments:

> A small degree of knowledge is not sufficient for a preacher of the Gospel. The sacred writings should be his treasure, and he should properly understand them. His knowledge does not consist in being furnished with a great

> variety of human learning ... (but) in being well instructed in the things concerning the kingdom of heaven, and the art of conducting men thither. Again, it is not enough for a man to have these advantages in possession: he must bring them forth, and distribute them abroad. A good pastor will not, like a miser, keep these things to himself to please his fancy; nor, like a merchant, traffic with them, to enrich himself; but, like a bountiful father or householder, distribute them with a liberal though judicious hand, for the comfort and support of the whole heavenly family.

Jesus commends his disciples as scribes (KJV) or students of Scripture (HCSB) instructed in the kingdom of heaven. They are learning so that they might teach. Old Testament figure Ezra, who prepared his heart to teach in Israel, is called a "scribe skilled in the law of Moses" (Ezra 7:6, 10), and Jesus' followers are to be like Ezra in knowledge and passion regarding the "old" and "new" treasures.

At the time of Ezra, and probably for some time after, the priests served a dual role as scholars, but over the course of time this changed. As the law grew in importance, its study and interpretation became a lifework by itself. So a new class of scholars arose: the scribes, who were not priests but who devoted themselves to the comprehensive study of the first five books of the Bible, the Pentateuch. During the Hellenistic period, the priests, especially the wealthier ones, were strongly influenced by Greek culture and turned their attention to pagan ideas. This aroused opposition by the scribes so that by the time of Christ, the scribes formed a distinct profession and held undisputed authority over the thoughts of the people. In the New Testament the scribes are called "students of Scripture," "experts in the law," and "teachers of the law" (see Matt. 13:52, 22:35; Luke 5:17, 7:30, 10:25, 11:45, 14:3; Acts 5:34).

Details

The "storeroom" also is known as the "treasury" or "place of deposit." It is a place not only for money, but for anything necessary for the comfort of the family. The Hebrew word *ostar* means depository, cellar, garner, store, or treasure-house, so it protects and preserves anything of value.[7] For the disciple of Jesus, the storeroom is the human heart—more specifically, the mind set on "what is above" (Col. 3:2) and the spirit yielded to Christ. Like the psalmist, believers are to treasure God's Word in their hearts so they will not sin (Psalms 119:11). But even more, they are to understand the deeper truths of Scripture so they may "contend for the faith" (Jude 3) and "always be ready to give a defense to anyone who asks you for a reason for the hope that is in you" (1 Peter 3:15).

Matthew Henry writes: "The instruction of a gospel minister must be in the kingdom of heaven, that is it about which his business lies. A man may be a great philosopher and politician, and yet if not instructed to the kingdom of heaven, he will make but a bad minister."

The treasures "new" and "old" are, of course, the understanding of the mystery of the kingdom of heaven in the context of the Old Testament. Jesus asked his disciples if they "understood all these things," to which they replied, "Yes" (Matt. 13:51). It is then that Jesus called them students of Scripture (scribes), likened them to landowners, and challenged them to reach deeply into their storeroom of understanding and proclaim the gospel of the kingdom. "Christ himself received that he might give; so must we, and we shall have more. In bringing forth, things new and old do best together; old truths, but new methods and expressions, especially new affections."[8]

Spiritual application

"Christ for three years gave instructions to the apostles; and they who preach should be able to understand the gospel; to defend it; and to communicate its truth to others. Human learning alone is indeed of no value to a minister; but all learning that will enable him better to

---

7   *International Standard Bible Encyclopedia.*
8   *Matthew Henry Unabridged.*

understand the Bible, and to communicate its truths, *is* valuable, and should, if possible, be gained. A minister should be like the father of a family: distributing to the church as it needs; and out of his treasures bringing forth truth to confirm the feeble, enlighten the ignorant, and guide those in danger of straying away."[9]

---

[9] *Barnes' Notes on the New Testament.*

Chapter 9

The Greatest in the Kingdom: The Parable of the Child

Matthew 18:1–9 (HCSB)

[1] At that time the disciples came to Jesus and said, "Who is greatest in the kingdom of heaven?"

[2] Then He called a child to Him and had him stand among them.

[3] "I assure you," He said, "unless you are converted and become like children, you will never enter the kingdom of heaven.

[4] Therefore, whoever humbles himself like this child—this one is the greatest in the kingdom of heaven.

[5] And whoever welcomes one child like this in My name welcomes Me.

[6] But whoever causes the downfall of one of these little ones who believe in Me—it would be better for him if a heavy millstone were hung around his neck and he were drowned in the depths of the sea!

[7] Woe to the world because of offenses. For offenses must come, but woe to that man by whom the offense comes.

[8] If your hand or your foot causes your downfall, cut it off and throw it away. It is better for you to enter life maimed or lame, than to have two hands or two feet and be thrown into the eternal fire.

⁹ And if your eye causes your downfall, gouge it out and throw it away. It is better for you to enter life with one eye, rather than to have two eyes and be thrown into hellfire!"

(See also Mark 9:33–50 and Luke 9:46–50)

The context

Jesus has been transfigured before Peter, James, and John. These three disciples emerge as the inner circle of Jesus' followers, with Peter declaring Jesus as Messiah (Matt. 16:16) and John being called "the one Jesus loved" (John 13:23). As Jesus and his disciples approach Capernaum, the disciples bicker about their place in the kingdom, which they still expect to be an imminent and earthly one. Knowing their hearts, Jesus asks, "What were you arguing about on the way?" (See Mark 9:33.) So they ask plainly, "Who is greatest in the kingdom of heaven?" (Matt. 18:1.)

Central theme

The central theme of this parable is that humility is highly valued in the kingdom of heaven. As the disciples struggle to understand the "mysteries" of the kingdom—especially that the kingdom is both a present reality and a future hope—they wonder about their role in it. Some would seek to sit at Jesus' right hand or left hand in the kingdom (Matt. 20:20–28), while others would desire to call fire down from heaven on those who refuse to welcome Jesus (Luke 9:51–56). Jesus calls a child and uses him to illustrate that such arrogant thinking has no place in the kingdom. Everyone must enter the kingdom as a child—humble, trusting, with no personal agenda—and once in the kingdom, no one should see himself or herself as more important than another. The entire value system of the kingdom of heaven is in stark contrast with that of Satan's kingdom and of this present evil age.

Central character

The child is the central character in this parable. Jesus calls a young boy and says, "[U]nless you are converted and become like children, you will never enter the kingdom of heaven" (Matt. 18:3). The word "converted" means changed or turned. It means to turn from one habit of life, or set of opinions, to another. Despite Jesus' teaching in previous parables, the disciples still seem to think the kingdom of heaven is coming imminently as an earthly kingdom. As a result, they jockey for positions in the king's cabinet. Jesus tells them they must turn from their wrong thinking about the kingdom and set aside their sinful ambition and pride.

In what way are the disciples to become like children? "Children are, to a great extent, destitute of ambition, pride, and haughtiness. They are characteristically humble and teachable. By requiring the disciples to be like them, he did not intend to express any opinion about the native moral character of children, but simply that *in these respects* they should become like them. They should lay aside their ambitious views, and pride, and be willing to occupy their proper station—a very lowly one."[10]

When Jesus says "whoever welcomes one *child like this* in My name welcomes Me" (Matt. 18:5) and "whoever causes the downfall of one of *these little ones* ..." (v. 6), he likely is referring not only to children but to new believers who are humble and teachable, and who need spiritual nurturing. The apostle John refers to Christians as "children" or "little children" (1 John 2:1, 12, 18, 28).

Details

In this teaching, Jesus addresses several facets of the kingdom: 1) entrance into the kingdom; 2) kingdom values; and 3) kingdom stewardship.

> **1) Entrance into the kingdom.** Jesus says, "[U]nless you are converted and become like children, you will never enter the kingdom of heaven" (Matt. 18:3). Entrance into the kingdom is by the new birth (John 3:3, 5), also known as regeneration, which is the work of the Holy Spirit imparting new life to the one who was "dead in ... trespasses and sins" (Eph. 2:1). No believer may take credit for the new birth but receives it with childlike wonder

---

10   Barnes' Notes on the New Testament.

and gratitude. In the same vein, no one may enter the narrow gate (Matt. 7:13) through arrogance or ambition; rather, eternal life is received in gracious humility. In light of these truths, and the disciples' boastful wrangling, Jesus challenges his followers to live like true citizens of the kingdom.

2) Kingdom values. Next, Jesus says, "Therefore, whoever humbles himself like this child—this one is the greatest in the kingdom of heaven" (Matt. 18:4). The things God values and the things people value are different. The values of the kingdom of Satan—summed up in 1 John 2:15–17 as "the lust of the flesh, the lust of the eyes, and the pride in one's lifestyle"— have no place in the kingdom of heaven and will be done away with in the end. It is wise for children of the kingdom to value what pleases the King.

3) Kingdom stewardship. Jesus, who has given his disciples the keys to the kingdom, warns them to be good stewards of it: "And whoever welcomes one child like this in My name welcomes Me. But whoever causes the downfall of one of these little ones who believe in Me—it would be better for him if a heavy millstone were hung around his neck and he were drowned in the depths of the sea" (Matt. 18:5–6). Millstones commonly are disc-shaped stones, two feet in diameter by six inches deep, used to grind grain. These millstones are turned by hand, but larger millstones are turned by mules. Binding millstones to people and casting them in the sea was one form of capital punishment practiced by the Greeks, Syrians, and Romans. It would be better to die in this way and escape everlasting consequences, Jesus says, than to keep another out of the kingdom or to neglect or mistreat the children of the kingdom. This is why Jesus tells the scribes and Pharisees they will receive greater damnation because they not only refuse to enter the kingdom but strive to keep others out (Matt. 23:13).

Finally, Jesus warns his disciples to beware of "offenses"—things that produce sin: "If your hand or your foot causes your downfall, cut it off and throw it away ... if your eye causes your downfall, gouge it out and throw it away ..." (Matt. 18:8–9). He is not teaching self mutilation, nor is he saying that in the resurrection some will have glorified bodies without hands, feet, or eyes. Rather, Jesus is teaching the flip side of the parables of the hidden treasure and the pearl of great price. While the kingdom is of inestimable value, the things of this world may keep us from entering in. As Richard Glover, quoted in *All the Parables of the Bible*, puts it, "The *hand* of ambitious rudeness should be cut off; the *eye* of ambitious coveting should be plucked out; the *foot* of ambitious willfulness should be cut off."

Matthew Henry provides further context: "Considering the cunning and malice of Satan, and the weakness and depravity of men's hearts, it is not possible but that there should be offences. God permits them for wise and holy ends, that those who are sincere, and those who are not, may be made known. Being told before, that there will be seducers, tempters, persecutors, and bad examples, let us stand on our guard. We must, as far as lawfully we may, part with what we cannot keep without being entangled by it in sin."

Spiritual application

Jesus calls believers "children of the kingdom" (Matt. 13:38, KJV) while the New Testament writers stress that we are adopted sons and daughters of God. As such, we are of most value to the kingdom when we trust God to provide our needs and serve him in simple, childlike faith. Pride has no place in the kingdom of heaven; Christ will abide no competitors to his sovereign Lordship.

Chapter 10

The King's Mercy: The Parable of the Unmerciful Servant

Matthew 18:21–35 (HCSB)

[21] Then Peter came to Him and said, "Lord, how many times could my brother sin against me and I forgive him? As many as seven times?"

[22] "I tell you, not as many as seven," Jesus said to him, "but 70 times seven.

[23] For this reason, the kingdom of heaven can be compared to a king who wanted to settle accounts with his slaves.

[24] When he began to settle accounts, one who owed 10,000 talents was brought before him.

[25] Since he had no way to pay it back, his master commanded that he, his wife, his children, and everything he had be sold to pay the debt.

[26] At this, the slave fell facedown before him and said, 'Be patient with me, and I will pay you everything!'

[27] Then the master of that slave had compassion, released him, and forgave him the loan.

[28] But that slave went out and found one of his fellow slaves who owed him 100 denarii. He grabbed him, started choking him, and said, 'Pay what you owe!'

²⁹ At this, his fellow slave fell down and began begging him, 'Be patient with me, and I will pay you back.'

³⁰ But he wasn't willing. On the contrary, he went and threw him into prison until he could pay what was owed.

³¹ When the other slaves saw what had taken place, they were deeply distressed and went and reported to their master everything that had happened.

³² Then, after he had summoned him, his master said to him, 'You wicked slave! I forgave you all that debt because you begged me.

³³ 'Shouldn't you also have had mercy on your fellow slave, as I had mercy on you?'

³⁴ And his master got angry and handed him over to the jailers until he could pay everything that was owed.

³⁵ So My heavenly Father will also do to you if each of you does not forgive his brother from his heart."

The context

Jesus is with his disciples and has been teaching them about humility. In Matthew 18:1, the disciples ask Jesus, "Who is greatest in the kingdom of heaven?" And in verses 2–9, he responds by calling over a child and telling his disciples that without childlike faith, no one may enter the kingdom. Further, he says that the one who humbles himself like a child is greatest in the kingdom; humility, not pride or performance, is most highly valued in the kingdom. Jesus is the ultimate example of humility, having set aside his heavenly glory to come to earth as the Suffering Servant. He reminds his disciples that the lost are of great value as he shares the parable of the lost sheep (verses 10–14), and he gives them instruction in the proper way to settle disagreements (verses 15–20). Now he turns his attention to Peter's question about how many times a disciple should forgive his brother. Jesus responds with the parable of the unmerciful servant.

Central theme

The central theme of this parable is that Christians take on the character of their Heavenly Father, who is merciful beyond human measure. Forgiveness is not a question of arithmetic; it's a matter of character. Peter asks, "Lord, how many times could my brother sin against me and I forgive him? As many as seven times?" He thinks he is being more gracious than the law requires. The Jews taught that a person was to forgive another three times, but not four. But Jesus' response—"70 times seven"—drives home the point that citizens of the kingdom naturally forgive others because much has been forgiven them.

Central character

The central character in this parable is the king who forgives a massive debt. The term is "myriads of talents," the highest number known in Greek arithmetical notation, according to commentator Adam Clarke. Depending on whether the talents are silver or gold, and whether they are Roman or Jewish coins, estimates of their current value range from $7.5 million to $150 million. In any case, it's a huge sum of money that one man could never repay.

The king is a picture of our Heavenly Father, who was so moved with compassion toward sinful mankind that he forgave our unfathomable sin debt by paying the price himself through his only Son (Rom. 5:8).

Details

The unmerciful servant likely is a tax collector. In ancient times, kings often farmed out, or sold for a price, the taxes of particular provinces. This ensured the king a known sum, but it also gave the tax collector in each province the opportunity to oppress his own people for personal gain. In this case, the servant no doubt was so dishonest that he denied the king his rightful cut. What a picture of the unbeliever. Matthew Henry comments: "He promises payment; Have patience awhile, and I will pay thee all. Note, It is the folly of many who are under convictions of sin, to imagine that they can make God satisfaction for the wrong they have done him ... He that had nothing to pay with (v. 25) fancied he could pay all. See how close pride sticks, even to awakened sinners; they are convinced, but not humbled."

The unpayable debt in this parable illustrates the enormity of our sins, which we are too impoverished to pay. According to Jewish law, debtors could be sold into servitude, along with their wives and children, until a family member redeemed them by paying the debt. But it is doubtful that any family had sufficient funds to pay off the massive debt this servant owed the king (see 2 Kings 4:1).

The forgiveness of the king represents God's justification, declaring us in right standing with him as he transfers our sin debt to his Son's account. Matthew Henry writes, "Every sin we commit is a debt to God … There is an account kept of these debts … some are more in debt, by reason of sin, than others … The God of infinite mercy is very ready, out of pure compassion, to forgive the sins of those that humble themselves before him."

The unmerciful servant, just loosed from his crushing debt, now confronts a fellow servant over what is likely a paltry debt and sends him to prison until the debt is paid. This so distresses the other slaves that they go to the king and report what has happened. The king, in turn, summons the unmerciful servant and turns him over to the "jailers/torturers/tormentors." Albert Barnes comments: "Torments were inflicted on *criminals*, not on debtors. They were inflicted by stretching the limbs, or pinching the flesh, or taking out the eyes, or taking off the skin while alive, etc. It is not probable that anything of this kind is intended, but only that the servant was punished by imprisonment till the debt should be paid."

So, does this mean God takes away a believer's justification if he or she does not forgive others? No. "This is not intended to teach us that God reverses his pardons to any, but that he denies them to those that are unqualified for them … Those that do not forgive their brother's trespasses did never truly repent of their own, and therefore that which is taken away is only what they seemed to have. This is intended to teach us, that they shall have judgment without mercy, that have showed no mercy" (James 2:13).[11] See also Matthew 6:14–15.

---

11   *Matthew Henry's Unabridged Commentary.*

Spiritual application

Having been pardoned of a sin debt we could never repay, citizens of the kingdom take on the character of their King and graciously forgive others of the wrongs against them. An unforgiving person demonstrates that he or she is not a true child of the King.

CHAPTER 11

The Servant's Charge: The Parable of the Vineyard Laborers

Matthew 20:1–16 (HCSB)

[1] "For the kingdom of heaven is like a landowner who went out early in the morning to hire workers for his vineyard.

[2] After agreeing with the workers on one denarius for the day, he sent them into his vineyard.

[3] When he went out about nine in the morning, he saw others standing in the marketplace doing nothing.

[4] To those men he said, 'You also go to my vineyard, and I'll give you whatever is right.' So off they went.

[5] About noon and at three, he went out again and did the same thing.

[6] Then about five he went and found others standing around, and said to them, 'Why have you been standing here all day doing nothing?'

[7] 'Because no one hired us,' they said to him. 'You also go to my vineyard,' he told them.

[8] When evening came, the owner of the vineyard told his foreman, 'Call the workers and give them their pay, starting with the last and ending with the first.'

⁹ When those who were hired about five came, they each received one denarius.

¹⁰ So when the first ones came, they assumed they would get more, but they also received a denarius each.

¹¹ When they received it, they began to complain to the landowner:

¹² 'These last men put in one hour, and you made them equal to us who bore the burden of the day and the burning heat!'

¹³ He replied to one of them, 'Friend, I'm doing you no wrong. Didn't you agree with me on a denarius?

¹⁴ Take what's yours and go. I want to give this last man the same as I gave you.

¹⁵ 'Don't I have the right to do what I want with my business? Are you jealous because I'm generous?'

¹⁶ So the last will be first, and the first last."

The context

Jesus is with his twelve disciples who have just witnessed his dealings with the rich young ruler and have heard his teaching that it is easier for a camel to pass through the eye of a needle than for a rich man to enter the kingdom of heaven. Startled, the disciples ask, "Then who can be saved?" Jesus responds, "With men this is impossible, but with God all things are possible." Peter points out that he and his fellow disciples have left everything to follow Jesus. "So what will there be for us?" he asks. Jesus assures Peter that everyone who has sacrificed for his name will be well compensated in the age to come. Jesus then closes out Matthew 19 by saying, "But many who are first will be last, and the last first" (v. 30), a phrase repeated in the parable that follows and gives us a key to understanding its meaning.

Central theme

The central theme of this parable is that all believers receive the complete reward of the kingdom. Commentaries suggest at least four possible interpretations:

1. This is a parable about the Gentiles who will enjoy the privileges of the new covenant, while the Jews, because of their rejection of the Messiah, will be set aside.

2. This is a parable about God's call to individual lives. The call early in the morning is for children; the call around nine is for youth; the call at noon is for adults; the call at three is for the aged; and the evening call is when sickness or other infirmities press hard on one's life.

3. This is a parable about the preaching of the gospel. The morning call is the preaching of John the Baptist; the second call is the preaching of Jesus; the third, the preaching of the fullness of the gospel after the ascension of Christ; the fourth, the mission of the apostles to the Jews; and the last call, the gospel presentation to the Gentiles.

4. This is a parable about humble Christian service. The followers of Christ should labor in his vineyard, the church, fully confident that they will receive their reward in heaven (see Matt. 5:12, 6:1; Luke 6:23). They need not be concerned that some have come into the kingdom before them, or after them, or that others' length of service or degree of giftedness is different from theirs.

The fourth interpretation of this parable seems to be the most faithful to the context. Consider what commentator Albert Barnes wrote in the early 1800s in *Barnes' Notes on the New Testament:*

> To all justice shall be done. To all to whom the rewards of heaven were promised, they shall be given. Nothing shall be withheld that was promised. If among this number who are called

into the kingdom I (God) choose to raise some to stations of distinguished usefulness, and to confer on them peculiar talents and higher rewards, I injure no other one. They shall enter heaven as was promised. If amidst the multitude of Christians, I choose to signalize such men as Paul, and Martyn, and Brainerd, and Spencer, and Summerfield—to appoint some of them to short labour, but to wide usefulness, and raise them to signal rewards—I injure not the great multitude of others who live long lives less useful, and less rewarded. All shall reach heaven, and all shall receive what I promise to the faithful.

Regarding Jesus' summary words, "So the last will be first, and the first last," F.F. Bruce comments, "What is the point of the saying in this context? It seems to be directed to the disciples and perhaps the point is that those who have given up most to follow Jesus must not suppose that the chief place in the kingdom of God is thereby granted to them."[12]

Herbert Lockyer adds, in *All the Parables of the Bible*, "As laborers may we ever remember that motive gives character to service, and that acceptable service is determined, not by duration, but by its spirit."

Central character

The central character in this parable is the landowner, a picture of Jesus who is Creator of all things (John 1:1–3; Col. 1:16), sovereign Lord over his creation, and the One to whom all judgment has been given (John 5:22). He actively and graciously seeks laborers for his vineyard, rewarding them justly for their work.

Details

In the immediate context, the laborers are Christ's disciples, who are among the first to labor in Christ's vineyard. The workers who come along later symbolize others—Jews and Gentiles—who will receive

---

12   *The Hard Sayings of Jesus, p. 199.*

The Kingdom According to Jesus

Christ and serve him throughout the church age. Matthew Henry comments, "God hires laborers, not because he needs them or their services … but as some charitable generous householders keep poor men to work, in kindness to them, to save them from idleness and poverty, and pay them for working for themselves."[13]

The *denarius* is the customary wage of a solider or a day laborer. The word is rendered "penny" in the King James Version.

The vineyard may be seen as the kingdom of heaven, into which people of all walks of life are called. Some would say the vineyard is the church, which requires constant pruning and care.

The marketplace may be seen as the world. The soul of man stands ready to be hired, for God made us to work. The devil seeks to hire people to waste their inheritance and feed swine, while the Lord calls them to dress his vineyard. We are put to the choice, for we must choose whom we will serve (Josh. 24:15).

It's important to note that some manuscripts add, "… for many are called, but few are chosen" to verse 16. Albert Barnes comments in *Barnes' Notes on the New Testament*:

> The meaning of this, in this connexion [sic], I take to be simply this: "Many are called into my kingdom; they come and labour as I command them; they are comparatively unknown and obscure; yet they are real Christians, and shall receive the proper reward. A few I have chosen for higher stations in the church. I have endowed them with apostolic gifts, or superior talents, or wider usefulness. They may not be so long in the vineyard; their race may be sooner run; but I have chosen to honour them in this manner; and I have a right to do it. I injure no one; and have a right to do what I will with mine own."

---

13   *Matthew Henry Unabridged.*

Rob Phillips

Spiritual application

As grateful laborers in Christ's vineyard, all believers should be faithful stewards of what God has entrusted to us, confident that we will receive our promised reward. At the same time, we should not be envious of those who may overtake us in length or fruitfulness of service.

CHAPTER 12

A Change of Ownership: The Parable of the Vineyard Owner

Matthew 21:33–46 (HCSB)

[33] "Listen to another parable: There was a man, a landowner, who planted a vineyard, put a fence around it, dug a winepress in it, and built a watchtower. He leased it to tenant farmers and went away.

[34] When the grape harvest drew near, he sent his slaves to the farmers to collect his fruit.

[35] But the farmers took his slaves, beat one, killed another, and stoned a third.

[36] Again, he sent other slaves, more than the first group, and they did the same to them.

[37] Finally, he sent his son to them. 'They will respect my son,' he said.

[38] But when the tenant farmers saw the son, they said among themselves, 'This is the heir. Come, let's kill him and take his inheritance!'

[39] So they seized him and threw him out of the vineyard, and killed him.

[40] Therefore, when the owner of the vineyard comes, what will he do to those farmers?"

⁴¹ "He will completely destroy those terrible men," they told Him, "and lease his vineyard to other farmers who will give him his produce at the harvest."

⁴² Jesus said to them, "Have you never read in the Scriptures: **The stone that the builders rejected has become the cornerstone. This came from the Lord and is wonderful in our eyes**?

⁴³ Therefore I tell you, the kingdom of God will be taken away from you and given to a nation producing its fruit."

⁴⁴ ["Whoever falls on this stone will be broken to pieces; but on whomever it falls, it will grind him to powder!"]

⁴⁵ When the chief priests and the Pharisees heard His parables, they knew He was speaking about them.

⁴⁶ Although they were looking for a way to arrest Him, they feared the crowds, because they regarded Him as a prophet.

This parable also appears in Mark 12:1–12 and Luke 20:9–19.

The context

Jesus has entered Jerusalem triumphantly on Palm Sunday. He has cleansed the temple complex, overturning the money changers' tables and driving out those who are turning the "house of prayer" into a "den of thieves" (Matt. 21:13). He has healed the blind and the lame and has received the praises of children. After spending the night in Bethany, he curses a fig tree on his way back to Jerusalem, and the tree—a symbol of Israel—withers at his words. Returning to the temple, Jesus is confronted by the chief priests and elders and challenged about his authority. He responds with a question about John the Baptist's baptism, whether it is from God or from men. When the Jewish leaders are not able to answer, Jesus tells the parable of the two sons, stating that "[T]ax collectors and prostitutes are entering the kingdom of God before you" (Matt. 21:31). He then tells the scathing parable of the vineyard owner, a parable so pointed that it prompts them to intensify their efforts to do away with him.

Central theme

The central theme of this parable is that the stewardship of the kingdom of heaven will be taken away from Israel and given to the church. Matthew Henry comments: "This parable plainly sets forth the sin and ruin of the Jewish nation; they and their leaders are the husbandmen here; and what is spoken for conviction to them, is spoken for caution to all that enjoy the privileges of the visible church, not to be high-minded, but fear."

Central characters

The central characters in this parable are the landowner and the vineyard. The landowner pictures God the Father, and the vineyard represents his kingdom on earth entrusted to the Jews. Note what God has done in establishing and furnishing the kingdom:

- He has planted the vineyard. God took the initiative to establish his kingdom on earth, a work of design and creation for which he assumed full responsibility.

- He has put a fence around it. God protected his kingdom from those who opposed it and sought to destroy it. As one commentator writes, "He will not have his vineyard to lie in common, that those who are without, may thrust in at pleasure; not to lie at large, that those who are within, may lash out at pleasure; but care is taken to set bounds about this holy mountain."[14]

- He has dug a winepress and built a tower. The altar was the winepress upon which atonement was made for man's sin and fellowship with God maintained; Mark's account refers to the pit under the press, where the wine gathered after being crushed out of the grapes. The watchtower was his constant vigilance over a nation and people he established to exalt his great name; some say this is the temple in which the divine presence is manifested.

---

14   *Matthew Henry Unabridged.*

In the context of this parable, God has carefully and lovingly established his kingdom on earth: a vineyard fully furnished to produce a great harvest to be richly enjoyed by God and his people.

Details

The owner leases out his vineyard to tenant farmers and goes away. This is a common practice in Jesus' day. The farmers occupy the vineyard, tend it, enjoy its fruits, and pay rent to the owner by sharing the harvest with him.

The tenant farmers in general are the Jews whom God has graciously and freely entrusted with his kingdom. To them, Paul says, "belong the adoption, the glory, the covenants, the giving of the law, the temple service, and the promises" (Rom. 9:4). God raised up the nation of Israel as the vehicle by which he would bless the whole world (Gen. 12:3). The farmers in particular are the Jewish religious leaders. Once God establishes the nation, reveals his purpose, gives the Jews the law, and provides a homeland for them, he goes away. This does not mean he abandons them; rather, it means there are fewer manifestations of his divine presence, while the law, prophets, and sacrificial system are given to the nation until the time of the harvest.

When the grape harvest "draws near," the landowner sends his servants—a common occurrence in which the tenant farmers share a portion of the harvest with the owner as rent. The servants in this case are the prophets who represent the master himself. But note how the tenants—especially the Jewish religious leaders—treat them: they beat one (scourge, flay, take off the skin), kill another, and stone a third. Those hearing the parable know full well that the Jews had beaten Jeremiah, killed Isaiah, and stoned Zechariah the son of Jehoiada in the temple. And when the Lord sends other servants, such as John the Baptist, they are imprisoned or beheaded.

At last, the master of the vineyard sends his son, whom "they will respect" (v. 37). But instead they recognize him as the heir, throw him out of the vineyard, and kill him. What a picture this is of the Jewish leaders who refuse to receive Jesus as Messiah, then take him outside of the city and crucify him. Matthew Henry comments: "Though the Roman power condemned him, yet it is still charged upon the chief priests and elders; for they were not only the prosecutors, but the principal agents, and had the greater sin."[15]

As Jesus finishes the story, he asks the Jewish leaders, "Therefore, when the owner of the vineyard comes, what will he do to those farmers?" They reply, "He will completely destroy those terrible men and lease his vineyard to other farmers who will give him his produce at the harvest" (v. 41). In effect, they have just condemned themselves and pronounced their own sentence. Within forty years of this parable, the Roman armies will sweep into Jerusalem, destroy the temple, kill more than one million Jews, and scatter the rest throughout the known world. The nation of Israel will cease to have its homeland and its center of worship for nearly 1,900 years, when national Israel is restored after the close of World War II; the Jewish people still await the rebuilding of the temple.

In contrast, a little over fifty days after this parable is told, the Holy Spirit comes on the day of Pentecost and ushers in the church age, taking up residence in the "temple" of the new believers' bodies (see 1 Cor. 6:19). Truly, God has temporarily set aside Israel and entrusted his kingdom to the church.

Jesus quotes Psalms 118:22–23 and alludes to Isaiah 8:14–15 when he says, "Have you never read the Scriptures: The stone that the builders rejected has become the cornerstone. This came from the Lord and is wonderful in our eyes" (v. 42)? Although many rejected Jesus, as a builder would reject one stone in favor of another, he would become the capstone, or cornerstone, of his new building, the church (see Acts 4:11; 1 Peter 2:7). Having referred to himself (not Peter) as the rock upon which the church would be built (Matt. 16:18), Jesus now states the consequences of coming into contact with him. "He that *runs against it*—a cornerstone, standing out from other parts of the foundation—shall be injured, or broken in his limbs or body. He that

---

15   *Matthew Henry Unabridged.*

is offended with *my* being the foundation, or that opposes me, shall, by the act, injure himself."[16]

Verse 44 is bracketed, meaning that some manuscripts omit it, but its imagery is significant. It's a reference to the custom of stoning as a punishment among the Jews. A scaffold is built, twice the height of the person to be stoned. Standing on the edge of the scaffold, the one being stoned is violently hit with a stone by one of the witnesses. If the person dies from the blow and the subsequent fall, nothing further is done; but if the person is resilient to the initial stoning, then a heavy stone is thrown down to crush and kill the accused—a stone so heavy it often required two men to lift it. "So the Saviour speaks of the falling of the stone on his enemies. They who oppose him, reject him, and continue impenitent, shall be crushed by him in the day of judgment, and perish for ever."[17] This also seems to allude to the crushing of the Jewish state by the Romans and the subsequent dispersion of the Jews through all the nations of the world.

The chief priests and Pharisees clearly understand that Jesus is directing this parable at them. Yet instead of repenting of their unbelief, they plot his arrest. Within a matter of days, the Jewish religious leaders will begin to fulfill the parable, and within a generation they will see it come to pass—first with the birthing of the church, then with the destruction of the Jewish temple and nation.

Spiritual application

Just as God set aside the nation of Israel due to its poor stewardship of his kingdom, he will not hesitate to chasten and rebuke those in his church who fail to be faithful stewards of his vineyard. "For the time has come for judgment to begin with God's household; and if it begins with us, what will the outcome be for those who disobey the gospel of God?" (1 Peter 4:17.)

---

16   *Barnes' Notes on the New Testament.*
17   *Barnes' Notes on the New Testament.*

CHAPTER 13

The King's Righteous Anger: The Parable of the Wedding Banquet

Matthew 22:1–14 (HCSB)

[1] Once more Jesus spoke to them in parables:

[2] "The kingdom of heaven may be compared to a king who gave a wedding banquet for his son.

[3] He sent out his slaves to summon those invited to the banquet, but they didn't want to come.

[4] Again, he sent out other slaves, and said, 'Tell those who are invited: Look, I've prepared my dinner; my oxen and fattened cattle have been slaughtered, and everything is ready. Come to the wedding banquet.'

[5] But they paid no attention and went away, one to his own farm, another to his business.

[6] And the others seized his slaves, treated them outrageously and killed them.

[7] The king was enraged, so he sent out his troops, destroyed those murderers, and burned down their city.

[8] Then he told his slaves, 'The banquet is ready, but those who were invited were not worthy.

⁹ Therefore, go to where the roads exit the city and invite everyone you find to the banquet.'

¹⁰ So those slaves went out on the roads and gathered everyone they found, both evil and good. The wedding banquet was filled with guests.

¹¹ But when the king came in to view the guests, he saw a man there who was not dressed for a wedding.

¹² So he said to him, 'Friend, how did you get in here without wedding clothes?' The man was speechless.

¹³ Then the king told the attendants, 'Tie him up hand and foot, and throw him into the outer darkness, where there will be weeping and gnashing of teeth.'

¹⁴ For many are invited, but few are chosen."

A similar parable is found in Luke 14:16–24.

The context

Jesus has made his triumphant entry into Jerusalem and cleansed the temple complex, driving out those who are buying and selling. He has received the praise of children and cursed the barren fig tree. He has answered the Pharisees' challenges to his authority and provided the parables of the two sons and the vineyard owner to illustrate the Jewish leaders' hardness of heart. Stung by Jesus' rebuke, they look for a way to arrest him.

Now, as Matthew 22 begins and Jesus' crucifixion draws near, he remains in the temple in the presence of the Pharisees and tells the parable of the wedding banquet.

Central theme

The central theme of this parable is that Israel will be judged for its rejection of the Messiah. The kingdom of heaven has been opened to the Gentiles—a joyous event the Jews should have anticipated and celebrated as friends of the King and his Son, the Bridegroom.

The Kingdom According to Jesus

Yet, because the generation of Jews witnessing Messiah's appearance has rejected him, God's wrath will fall upon them. This prophecy is fulfilled in 70 AD.

Central character

The central character in this parable is the king, who represents God the Father. He chooses the nation of Israel as his own special people, and invites them to the wedding of his Son through the prophets. Yet their hearts grow hard, and when the time comes for the Son of God to appear, they will not receive him. Therefore, the Jews are set aside as the Gentiles are welcomed in.

Details

The wedding banquet, in all likelihood, is an evening meal. In Jewish culture, two invitations are sent out. The first asks the guests to attend, and the second announces that all is ready and provides the time at which the guests are to arrive. In this story, the king offers a third invitation, but the invited guests respond by treating the king's slaves cruelly—even killing them. There is little doubt that the banquet is a picture of the covenant fellowship between Christ (the king's son) and the church (his bride) in the current age. The Jews under the old covenant are the invited guests who disregard the Father's invitation, treat his slaves (the prophets) cruelly, and despise his Son. There also is a sense in which this refers not only to Jews, but to all people and cultures that have closed their eyes to the light of the promised Messiah.

"The king was enraged," according to verse 7, "so he sent out his troops, destroyed those murderers, and burned down their city." This is Jesus' prophecy of the judgment that would befall the nation of Israel in 70 AD, when the Roman armies under Titus sacked Jerusalem, completely destroyed the temple, killed more than one million Jews, and scattered the rest of the Jewish nation. Jesus also speaks of this terrible day in Matthew 24:1–2.

Now the king directs his slaves to go "where the roads exit the city and invite everyone you find to the banquet" (v. 9). Luke adds the word "hedges" or "lanes" (Luke 14:23) "to point out the people to whom the apostles were sent, as either miserable vagabonds, or the most indigent poor, who were wandering about the country, or sitting by the sides of the ways and hedges, imploring relief. This verse points out the final rejection of the Jews, and the calling of the Gentiles."[18]

So the slaves fill the banquet hall with "everyone they found, both evil and good" (v. 10), a picture of the visible, or professing, church. Scripture is abundantly clear that not everyone who claims the name of Jesus truly knows him, despite appearances to the contrary (Matt. 7:21–23). In the same way, the church throughout this present evil age will consist of professors and possessors—those who profess to know Christ and those who truly have his Spirit within them as the distinguishing mark of the true believer (Rom. 8:9).

Next we come to the guest "who was not dressed for a wedding" (v. 11). In ancient times, kings and princes provided fresh clothing to their guests. Normally these were long white robes. To refuse such gifts, or to appear at the banquet without them, was an expression of highest contempt. Albert Barnes comments in his *Notes on the New Testament*:

> This beautifully represents the conduct of the hypocrite in the church. A garment of salvation might be his, wrought by the hands of the Saviour, and dyed in his blood. But the hypocrite chooses the filthy rags of his own righteousness, and thus offers the highest contempt for that provided in the gospel. He is to blame, not for being invited; not for coming, if he would come—for he is freely invited; but for offering the highest contempt to the King of Zion, in presenting himself with all his filth and rags, and in refusing to be saved in the way provided in the gospel.

The king confronts the guest in verse 12: "Friend [*companion* is a better term], how did you get in here without wedding clothes?" The man is speechless—"muzzled, or gagged," according to *Adam Clarke's Commentary*. Just as the guest is silenced by his own conscience, the

---

18   *Adam Clarke's Commentary.*

unbeliever will stand before God one day "without excuse" (Rom. 1:20). As a result, the king orders his guest to be bound hand and foot and thrown into "the outer darkness," away from the fellowship of the wedding party, perhaps even into a dungeon. In a similar way, Christ will cast unbelievers out of his kingdom into everlasting punishment on the day they are summoned before the great white throne (Rev. 20:11–15; see also Matt. 7:21–3; 8:12; 25:30).

"It will aggravate their misery, that ... they shall see all this plenty with their eyes, but shall not taste of it," writes Matthew Henry. "Hell is utter darkness, it is darkness out of heaven, the land of light; or it is extreme darkness, darkness to the last degree, without the least ray or spark of light, or hope of it, like that of Egypt; darkness which might be felt ... Hypocrites go by the light of the gospel itself down to utter darkness; and hell will be hell indeed to such, a condemnation more intolerable; there shall be weeping, and gnashing of teeth."[19]

Finally we come to the phrase Jesus uses often in the Gospels, "For many are invited [called], but few are chosen" (v. 14). This is an allusion to the Roman method of raising an army. All men are mustered, but only those fit for duty are chosen to serve. Many are invited to the wedding feast, but most ignore the invitation, make light of it, find themselves otherwise engaged in worldly matters, abuse the King's messengers, or show up in the filthy rags of their own righteousness; a comparatively small number enter the kingdom through the narrow gate (Matt. 7:13–14).

Spiritual application

To enter the fellowship of the King we must make sure we are clothed in the righteousness of Christ—true possessors of the Holy Spirit and not merely professors of the faith.

---

[19]   *Matthew Henry Unabridged.*

CHAPTER 14

The King's Delayed Return: The Parable of the Ten Virgins

Matthew 25:1–13

[1] "Then the kingdom of heaven will be like 10 virgins who took their lamps and went out to meet the groom.

[2] Five of them were foolish and five were sensible.

[3] When the foolish took their lamps, they didn't take oil with them.

[4] But the sensible ones took oil in their flasks with their lamps.

[5] Since the groom was delayed, they all became drowsy and fell asleep.

[6] In the middle of the night there was a shout: 'Here's the groom! Come out to meet him.'

[7] Then all those virgins got up and trimmed their lamps.

[8] But the foolish ones said to the sensible ones, 'Give us some of your oil, because our lamps are going out.'

[9] The sensible ones answered, 'No, there won't be enough for us and for you. Go instead to those who sell, and buy oil for yourselves.'

[10] When they had gone to buy some, the groom arrived. Then those who were ready went in with him to the wedding banquet, and the door was shut.

¹¹ Later the rest of the virgins also came and said, 'Master, master, open up for us!'

¹² But he replied, 'I assure you: I do not know you!'

¹³ Therefore be alert, because you don't know either the day or the hour."

The context

Jesus is on the Mount of Olives with his disciples, responding to their questions about the future destruction of the temple and the end of the age. Just before this, in Matthew 23, Jesus pronounces woes on the Jewish leaders for their hypocrisy. Then, leaving the temple and crossing over the Kidron Valley, he tells his disciples that the temple, a glistening monument to Jewish nationalism (but a stale house of worship where he was rejected as Messiah), would soon be demolished. Shocked by this prediction, his disciples ask him in Matthew 24:3, "When will these things happen (the destruction of the temple)? And what is the sign of your coming and of the end of the age?" Jesus responds in the rest of Matthew 24–25 in what is known as the Olivet Discourse. The parable of the ten virgins comes in the middle of this message.

Central theme

The central theme of this parable is that people should stay alert and be prepared for the return of Christ.

Central character

The central character in this parable is the bridegroom, or Christ, who is delayed in his coming for the bride, the church. Scripture often refers to the church as the bride and Christ as the bridegroom (Matt. 9:15; Mark 2:19–20; Luke 5:34–35; John 3:29). Believers are "espoused" or "betrothed" to Jesus, who promises he will come one day and take them to his Father's house (John 14:1–3).

An understanding of the Jewish wedding custom is helpful in navigating this parable. In Jesus' day, if a young man has acquired sufficient means to provide a marriage dowry—or payment for a bride—then his parents select a girl for him, call in a "friend of the bridegroom" (John 3:29) to represent them, and begin negotiations with the bride's father, who also selects a representative. If consent is given for the bride to be married, and if there is agreement on the amount to be paid, congratulations are exchanged, coffee is brought out, and everyone drinks as a seal of the marriage covenant. Later, the families of the bride and groom meet. The young man gives the young woman a gold ring, some article of value, or simply a document in which he promises to marry her, saying, "See by this ring (or this token) thou art set apart for me, according to the law of Moses and of Israel." The young man then leaves his bride-to-be, promising to return once he has prepared a place for her.

He then returns to his father's home and, under his father's supervision, prepares a wedding chamber for his bride. The period of betrothal normally lasts a year or more and may only be broken by obtaining a bill of divorcement. While the bridegroom works on the wedding chamber, the bride prepares herself for the wedding and remains chaste—covering her face with a veil in public to show she is pledged to be married.

At last, the father gives word to his son that all is ready and the night of the wedding arrives. The groom dresses as much like a king as possible. If he is wealthy enough, he wears a gold crown; otherwise, it is a garland of fresh flowers. The bride, meanwhile, goes through an elaborate and costly adorning. Every effort is made to make her complexion glossy and shining like marble. Her dark locks of hair are braided with gold and pearls, and she is decked with all the precious stones and jewels her family has inherited from previous generations.

The groom sets out from his father's house to the home of the bride in a nighttime procession attended by wedding guests bearing torches. The bride steps out to meet him, receives the blessing of her relatives, and then proceeds across town with the groom to his father's home. A grand procession follows them. The invited guests who did not go to the bride's home are allowed to join the march along the way and go with the whole group to the marriage feast. Since the streets are dark, the guests require the light of a torch or lamp, without which they may not join the procession or enter the feast.

There are demonstrations of joy all along the route. Family members hand out ears of parched grain to the children, musical instruments are played, and there is dancing and shouts of "Behold, the bridegroom comes!" At last they reach the home of the bridegroom's father, where the specially built wedding chamber is prepared. Together they enter the suite and shut the door, and for seven days they stay inside, alone. Meanwhile, a seven-day celebration breaks out. At the end of the seven days, the bride and groom emerge, leave the father's house, and set out to establish their own home.

This is the context in which Jesus' disciples hear the parable, so the truths about the bridegroom going away, preparing a place, and returning are well-known, as are the elements of delay and surprise. This parable clearly is a teaching that Jesus, after his suffering, death, and resurrection, would return to his Father, prepare a place in heaven for believers, and then call his bride to meet him in the air in an event known as the rapture (1 Cor. 15:50–57; 1 Thess. 4:13–18). The seven-day honeymoon perhaps depicts the seven years the church is in heaven while the tribulation takes place on earth. And the leaving of the father's house after the honeymoon may picture the glorious appearing of Christ when he returns to earth with the saints, sitting on the throne of David, and ruling the earth with his bride.

Details

It is interesting to note that the bride is not mentioned in this parable. While Scripture often refers to Christ's church as his bride, the focus in this parable is on the bridegroom and the virgins, or attendants. It is not necessary for believers to be represented as both bride and bridal attendants, or this would present difficulties Jesus did not intend. Remember that his parables generally illustrate one key spiritual truth—and this parable warns all those who profess Christianity to make sure they are ready for Christ's return.

Therefore, let's see the virgins as professors of the faith, those who claim to know the Bridegroom and await his coming. Some are "wise" and some are "foolish"—not good and bad. There is at least a degree of goodwill, and good intentions, in the foolish as well as in the wise. The difference is in the depth of their commitment, which is evident by their readiness for the Bridegroom's coming.

The wise virgins are those who truly know Christ and are known by him. They understand that his coming may be delayed, so they are prepared with an abundance of oil, "that *inward reality of grace* which alone will stand when He appears whose eyes are as a flame of fire."[20] They may not be excused for slumbering while the Bridegroom tarries—even Christ's closest followers could not stay awake one hour while he prayed in the Garden of Gethsemane—yet they persevere and are allowed into the marriage feast.

The foolish virgins are those who profess to know Christ but lack a genuine relationship with him. They carry their lamps—an outward profession of their faith in the Messiah—but they lack the reserve of oil that is the indwelling presence of the Holy Spirit. When the Bridegroom comes, their lamps are dark.

The supply of oil may be seen as the inward grace of Christ that has enduring character. Whereas God's grace is given to all in a general sense, only those who have entered into a relationship with him receive his Spirit who, like the oil of the wise, is abundant and sufficient.

Nothing should be made of the fact that there are ten virgins, other than that Jews would not hold synagogue, a wedding, or another ceremony without at least ten witnesses. The fact that five of the virgins are wise and five are foolish should not be taken to mean that half of all professing Christians are lost. There is folly in reading too much into the details of Christ's parables.

All ten of the virgins "slumbered and slept." The word "slumbered" signifies "nodding off" or "becoming drowsy." The word "slept" is the usual word for lying down to sleep. This denotes two states of spiritual stupor. First, "that half-involuntary lethargy or drowsiness which is apt to steal over one who falls into inactivity; and then a conscious, deliberate yielding to it, after a little vain resistance."[21]

20   *Jamieson-Fausset-Brown Bible Commentary.*
21   *Jamieson-Fausset-Brown Bible Commentary.*

The lamps are of two general kinds. The first consists of rags wrapped around one end of a wooden pole and dipped in oil. The second, and most likely, consists of a "round receptacle for pitch or oil for the wick. This was placed in a hollow cup or deep saucer ... which was fastened by a pointed end into a long wooden pole, on which it was born aloft."[22]

When the bridegroom comes at last, the foolish virgins need oil, for their lamps are going out, and so they ask the wise for oil. The response of the wise is important in two respects. First, they deny the request for oil—not out of selfishness or a judgmental nature, but because all ten virgins would then be undone. Salvation is not to be acquired from believers but from God. Second, the wise virgins tell the foolish to buy their own reserve of oil. This does not imply that salvation may be purchased, only that the foolish need to acquire salvation the same way the wise did.

When the bridegroom comes, the wise are ready. They join the wedding procession with their blazing lamps and are welcomed in. The foolish come too late, after the door has been shut, and are excluded from the wedding feast. Today, believers and unbelievers populate the visible church; in a day to come, God will separate those who merely profess to know Christ from those who truly do.

Spiritual application

There is no improving on the words of Jesus, "Therefore be alert, because you don't know either the day or the hour" when the Bridegroom will come (Matt. 25:13).

---

[22] *Dr. Alfred Edersheim, quoted in Manners and Customs of Bible Lands.*

CHAPTER 15

The Separation of the Righteous from the Wicked: The Parable of the Sheep and Goats

Matthew 25:31–46 (HCSB)

[31] "When the Son of Man comes in His glory, and all the angels with Him, then He will sit on the throne of His glory.

[32] All the nations will be gathered before Him, and He will separate them one from another, just as a shepherd separates the sheep from the goats.

[33] He will put the sheep on His right and the goats on the left.

[34] Then the King will say to those on His right, 'Come, you who are blessed by My Father, inherit the kingdom prepared for you from the foundation of the world.

[35] For I was hungry and you gave Me something to eat; I was thirsty and you gave Me something to drink; I was a stranger and you took Me in;

[36] I was naked and you clothed Me; I was sick and you took care of Me; I was in prison and you visited Me.'

[37] Then the righteous will answer Him, 'Lord, when did we see You hungry and feed You, or thirsty and give You something to drink?

⁳⁸ When did we see You a stranger and take You in, or without clothes and clothe You?

³⁹ When did we see You sick, or in prison, and visit You?'

⁴⁰ And the King will answer them, 'I assure you: Whatever you did for one of the least of these brothers of Mine, you did for Me.'

⁴¹ Then He will also say to those on the left, 'Depart from Me, you who are cursed, into the eternal fire prepared for the Devil and his angels!

⁴² For I was hungry and you gave Me nothing to eat; I was thirsty and you gave Me nothing to drink;

⁴³ I was a stranger and you didn't take Me in; I was naked and you didn't clothe Me, sick and in prison and you didn't take care of Me.'

⁴⁴ Then they too will answer, 'Lord, when did we see You hungry, or thirsty, or a stranger, or without clothes, or sick, or in prison, and not help You?'

⁴⁵ Then He will answer them, 'I assure you: Whatever you did not do for one of the least of these, you did not do for Me either.'

⁴⁶ And they will go away into eternal punishment, but the righteous into eternal life."

The context

This parable ends the so-called Olivet Discourse of Matthew 24–25. Jesus is on the Mount of Olives with his disciples, responding to their questions about the future destruction of the temple and the end of the age: "When will these things happen (the destruction of the temple)? And what is the sign of your coming and of the end of the age" (Matt. 24:3)? He concludes his teaching in Matthew 25 with an exhortation to watchfulness (the parable of the ten virgins, Matt. 25:1–13); an encouragement to faithfulness (the parable of the talents, Matt. 25:14–30); and an assurance of righteous judgment (the parable of the sheep and goats, Matt. 25:31–46).

Central theme

The central theme of this parable is that Christ will separate believers from unbelievers at his return.

Central character

The central character in this parable is Christ, who assures his disciples he will return one day with the holy angels and sit on the throne of his glory, "the glory of His judicial authority."[23] Jesus refers to himself as a shepherd who faithfully separates the sheep from the goats. Jesus knows who belongs to him and who does not. "My sheep hear My voice, I know them, and they follow Me," he says in John 10:27. There are many other references to God/Christ as the shepherd and to his followers as sheep (see Ps. 23:1, 80:1; Zech. 13:7; Matt. 26:31; John 10:11, 14, 16; Heb. 13:20; 1 Peter 2:25, 5:4). In this parable, Jesus plainly teaches that a time of separation is coming when those who are of his flock will enjoy the benefits of his kingdom while those who have rejected him will be rejected themselves.

Details

It's important to establish *when* this judgment takes place and *who* it involves as the sheep and goats. There is considerable disagreement over these two questions. Some commentators believe this parable is a general description of the final judgment of all mankind—a summary of both the judgment seat of Christ for believers (Rom. 14:10; 2 Cor. 5:10) and the great white throne judgment for unbelievers (Rev. 20:11–15), even though these judgments may be separated by a thousand years or more. Other scholars, however, believe this parable teaches a separate judgment for all those who survive the great tribulation and witness the return of Christ.

In the context of Jesus' teaching on the Mount of Olives in Matthew 24–25, and since there is no reference to resurrection, it appears Jesus will carry out this judgment in concert with his personal, physical, and glorious return one day, and that the sheep and goats represent those who are alive at his return. Their treatment of "the least of these

---

23   *Jamieson-Fausset-Brown Bible Commentary.*

brothers of Mine" (Matt. 25:40) indicates the true condition of their hearts, either as believers in Christ or rejecters of the King of Kings and Lord of Lords.

Next, it's helpful to look more closely at some key words and phrases Jesus uses in this parable:

- **Son of Man.** This is the name Jesus most frequently gives to himself. "Some eighty times He thus designated Himself and this familiar title was a racial one as the representative Man."[24] Used also in the Old Testament, this term has Messianic meaning, and by using it liberally, Jesus is revealing not only his identity with man (John 1:14) but his identity as the Son of God.

- **All the nations.** The word "nations" also may be translated "Gentiles." Herbert Lockyer points out in *All the Parables of the Bible* that "when the plural is used in the Bible, it represents all the heathen or Gentile nations of the world as distinguished from the Jewish nation." Others argue that the Jews are necessarily included here. Still others teach that this is a reference to representatives of all the sovereign nations of the world, which will be judged for their treatment of God's people as all national boundaries are dissolved. It seems best in the context of this parable to see the nations/Gentiles as those individuals who are alive at the glorious appearing of Christ.

- **Sheep and goats.** These creatures often graze together, and it takes the trained eye of the shepherd to separate them at the time of shearing. Sheep symbolize mildness, simplicity, innocence—the qualities of one completely dependent upon the shepherd for protection and care. Clearly, these are believers. Goats naturally are quarrelsome, selfish and smelly—a stark contrast that highlights the profane and impure character of unbelievers.

- **Right and left.** "The right hand is the place of honour, and denotes the situation of those who are honoured, or those who

---

24   Herbert Lockyer, All the Parables of the Bible.

are virtuous ... The left was the place of dishonour, denoting condemnation."[25]

- **The King.** This is the only time Jesus directly refers to himself as King—and just three days before he is crucified as a common criminal.

- **Brothers of mine.** Some teach that these are the Jews, and eternal rewards await those who care for God's chosen people, especially throughout the great tribulation. Others believe this is a reference to all believers. It would appear this phrase describes those who trust in Christ—at great personal cost—during the period between the rapture of the church and the glorious appearing of the King.

Now, let's look more closely at what Jesus says to those who stand before him in judgment. To those on his right, he says, "Come, you who are blessed by My Father, inherit the kingdom prepared for you from the foundation of the world" (v. 34). Believers often are called heirs of God and/or co-heirs with Christ in Scripture (see Rom. 8:17; Gal. 4:6–7; Heb. 1:14). The kingdom of heaven has been "prepared"—designed, appointed—for believers from the beginning. This is no new plan; rather, it is the fulfillment of God's eternal plan to bless his own.

What is the basis of this blessing for these people? "For I was hungry and you gave Me something to eat; I was thirsty and you gave Me something to drink; I was a stranger and you took Me in; I was naked and you clothed Me; I was sick and you took care of Me; I was in prison and you visited Me" (vv. 35–36). We know from Jesus' own words that eternal life is received by faith and not by works (John 5:24). So what he seems to be saying is that the way the sheep treat God's children demonstrates that they truly know him. "The surprise expressed is not at their being told that they acted from love to Christ, but that Christ Himself was the Personal Object of all their deeds."[26]

In contrast, Jesus says to those on his left, "Depart from Me, you who are cursed, into the eternal fire prepared for the Devil and his angels" (v. 41). The one who rejects Christ is "already condemned, because

---

25 *Barnes' Notes on the New Testament.*
26 *Jamieson-Fausset-Brown Bible Commentary.*

he has not believed in the name of the One and Only Son of God" (John 3:18). According to *Barnes' Notes on the New Testament*, "There is a remarkable difference between the manner in which the righteous shall be addressed, and the wicked. Christ will say to the one that the kingdom was prepared for *them*; to the other, that the fire was not prepared for *them*, but for another race of beings. They will inherit it because they have the same character as the devil, and therefore are fitted to the same place."

What is the basis of this departure into eternal fire? "For I was hungry and you gave Me nothing to eat; I was thirsty and you gave Me nothing to drink; I was a stranger and you didn't take Me in; I was naked and you didn't clothe Me, sick and in prison and you didn't take care of Me" (vv. 42–43). As with the sheep, the goats' destiny is not determined by works; rather, the works demonstrate the true condition of the heart. The unbeliever does not care for heirs of the kingdom because he has no regard for the King. And so, by his choice, the goat departs into eternal fire.

Spiritual application

Our acts of kindness, especially toward those "who belong to the household of faith" (Gal. 6:10), demonstrate our true nature as children of the King, and are received by Christ as if done for him personally.

CHAPTER 16

The Lord of the Harvest: The Parable of the Growing Seed

Mark 4:26–29 (HCSB)

²⁶ "The kingdom of God is like this," He said. "A man scatters seed on the ground;

²⁷ he sleeps and rises—night and day, and the seed sprouts and grows—he doesn't know how.

²⁸ The soil produces a crop by itself—first the blade, then the head, and then the ripe grain on the head.

²⁹ But as soon as the crop is ready, he sends for the sickle, because harvest has come."

The context

Mark is the only gospel writer to record this parable, which Jesus tells after explaining the parable of the sower to his disciples (Mark 4:13–20) and after admonishing them to share his teachings with others (Mark 4:21–25). Commentators like Herbert Lockyer believe this parable "can be regarded as supplementary to the parable of *The Sower*, being designed to complete the history of the growth of the good seed which fell on the good ground. It is one of the three parables which reveal the mysteries of the Kingdom of God in terms of a sower's work."[27]

---
27 *All the Parables of the Bible.*

Central theme

The central theme of this parable is that God is sovereign over his kingdom. Christ's disciples are to labor faithfully in his fields, but it is God who gives the growth (see 1 Cor. 3:5–8).

Central character

The central character in this parable is the man who "scatters seed on the ground" (Mark 4:26). This represents all those whom God uses to establish his kingdom in the hearts of men. Christ has finished the work of redemption and has given to his followers the responsibility of carrying the gospel message to the entire world (Matt. 28:19–20; Mark 16:15). God the Father draws people to Christ and grants them everlasting life through the mysterious work of the Holy Spirit, bringing the spiritually dead to new life in Christ. As Matthew Henry writes, "… we know not how the Spirit by the word makes a change in the heart, any more than we can account for the blowing of the wind, which we hear the sound of, but cannot tell whence it comes, or whither it goes."[28] On this side of heaven, believers will never fully understand how God works to populate his kingdom, yet we are called to faithfully spread the good news of the kingdom (Matt. 4:23, 9:35, 24:14; Mark 1:14).

Details

According to Herbert Lockyer in *All the Parables of the Bible*, "Our Lord was directing His disciples to the three stages of *The Kingdom of God*":

1. The blade, or the kingdom in mystery (the church age)

2. The ear, or the kingdom in manifestation throughout the millennial kingdom

3. The full corn, or the kingdom in its majestic perfection after God creates new heavens and a new earth

While other commentators apply this parable to the believer's personal spiritual growth, Lockyer's interpretation seems to fit Jesus' other

---

28   *Matthew Henry Unabridged.*

The Kingdom According to Jesus

parables of the kingdom of heaven. The Jews in Jesus' day are expecting the kingdom to come in a singular, dramatic event. Yet Jesus teaches through his parables that the kingdom of heaven is both a present reality and a future hope, growing to full maturity over a long period of time.

Let's look more closely at other elements in this parable:

- **The seed.** Most certainly this is "the living and enduring word of God" (1 Peter 1:23). As Jesus explains following the parable of the sower, "The seed is the word of God" (Luke 8:11)—the good news that the kingdom has come in the person of Jesus the Messiah and that all may enter into the kingdom by faith in him, the Word (*Logos*, John 1:1).

- **The ground.** As in the parable of the sower, the ground symbolizes the human heart. The ground cannot sow and it cannot reap, but it may receive the seed. The starting place of the kingdom of heaven is the heart captivated by God. When Jesus says that "the soil produces a crop by itself" (v. 28) we are not required "to suppose that our Saviour meant to say that the earth had any productive power by itself, but only that it produced its fruits not by the power of man. God gives it its power ... So religion in the heart is not by the *power* of man."[29]

- **The mystery of the growth.** The sower sleeps, rises, and does not know how the seed bursts forth into life and fruitfulness. In the same way, we do not understand the mysterious work of God in the hearts of men and women. Nor can we fully fathom his work in bringing the kingdom to full maturity. "For My thoughts are not your thoughts, and your ways are not My ways ... For as heaven is higher than earth, so My ways are higher than your ways, and My thoughts than your thoughts" (Isa. 55:8–9).

- **The harvest.** This may be looked upon as the consummation of all things (Matt. 13:39)—"the most glorious consummation

---

29   *Barnes' Notes on the New Testament.*

when with the devil forever vanquished, and sin completely destroyed, and the emergence of a new heaven and a new earth, Jesus will surrender all things to the Father."[30]

Spiritual application

Just as Christ's kingdom will grow to full maturity, God's design for his children is that "we all reach unity in the faith and in the knowledge of God's Son, [growing]into a mature man with a stature measured by Christ's fullness" (Eph. 4:13).

---

30   *All the Parables of the Bible.*

CHAPTER 17

The Call to Accountability: The Parable of the Ten Minas

Luke 19:11–27

[11] As they were listening to this, He went on to tell a parable because He was near Jerusalem, and they thought the kingdom of God was going to appear right away.

[12] Therefore He said: "A nobleman traveled to a far country to receive for himself authority to be king and then return.

[13] He called 10 of his slaves, gave them 10 minas, and told them, 'Engage in business until I come back.'

[14] But his subjects hated him and sent a delegation after him, saying, 'We don't want this man to rule over us!'

[15] At his return, having received the authority to be king, he summoned those slaves he had given the money to so he could find out how much they had made in business.

[16] The first came forward and said, 'Master, your mina has earned 10 more minas.'

[17] 'Well done, good slave!' he told him. 'Because you have been faithful in a very small matter, have authority over 10 towns.'

[18] The second came and said, 'Master, your mina has made five minas.'

[19] So he said to him, 'You will be over five towns.'

[20] And another came and said, 'Master, here is your mina. I have kept it hidden away in a cloth

[21] because I was afraid of you, for you're a tough man: you collect what you didn't deposit and reap what you didn't sow.'

[22] He told him, 'I will judge you by what you have said, you evil slave! [If] you knew I was a tough man, collecting what I didn't deposit and reaping what I didn't sow,

[23] why didn't you put my money in the bank? And when I returned, I would have collected it with interest!'

[24] So he said to those standing there, 'Take the mina away from him and give it to the one who has 10 minas.'

[25] But they said to him, 'Master, he has 10 minas.'

[26] 'I tell you, that to everyone who has, more will be given; and from the one who does not have, even what he does have will be taken away.

[27] But bring here these enemies of mine, who did not want me to rule over them, and slaughter them in my presence.'"

A similar parable appears in Matt. 25:14–30. Yet these parables differ in several respects. The parable in Matthew is spoken *after* Jesus enters Jerusalem; the parable in Luke is shared while he is on his way there. The parable in Matthew is delivered on the Mount of Olives; the parable in Luke is given in the home of Zacchaeus. Finally, the parable in Matthew is delivered to teach Jesus' followers the necessity of improving the talents committed to them; the parable in Luke focuses primarily on correcting the false notion that the kingdom of heaven would immediately appear.

The Kingdom According to Jesus

The context

Jesus is passing through Jericho and has dined in the home of Zacchaeus, chief of the tax collectors, amidst grumblings from onlookers that "He's gone to lodge with a sinful man" (Luke 19:7). Upon Zacchaeus' declaration of repentance, Jesus announces that salvation has come to his home, consistent with his words to the chief priests and elders in Matthew 21:31 that "tax collectors and prostitutes are entering the kingdom of God before you!" Now, with the crowds listening and thinking that "the kingdom of God (is) going to appear right away" (v. 11), Jesus tells the parable of the ten minas.

Central theme

The central theme of this parable is that the kingdom of heaven will come in its fullness at a later time. Jesus' followers "thought the kingdom of God was going to appear right away" (v. 11). His parable corrects that shortsighted view. At the same time, the central theme feeds two other truths: first, the Jews would be judged for their rejection of the Messiah; and second, the King would hold his servants accountable for their stewardship.

The day is coming when all believers must "stand before the judgment seat of Christ" (Rom. 14:10, KJV). At that time, "each may be repaid for what he has done in the body, whether good or bad" (2 Cor. 5:10). The apostle Paul writes that this judgment is like a fire that refines good works and consumes dead works (see 1 Cor. 3:11–15). For faithful believers who wisely use all that God has entrusted to them while he is in "a far country," they will receive rewards, referred to throughout the New Testament as "crowns" (see 1 Cor. 9:25; Phil. 4:1; 1 Thess. 2:19; 2 Tim. 4:8; James 1:12; 1 Peter 5:4; Rev. 2:10).

Central character

The central character in this parable is the nobleman who leaves the country to receive authority to be king and then returns. This clearly represents Christ, who tells his disciples he must "go away" (John 16:7) but promises to return (John 14:3). Like the nobleman who is "hated" by his subjects who send a delegation after him saying, "We don't want this man to rule over us" (v. 14), Jesus is "despised and rejected by men" (Isa. 53:3). Further, "He came to His own, and His own people did not receive Him" (John 1:11). Jesus gives his listeners a clear message that the kingdom cannot come in its fullness until he completes the work of salvation and goes to his Father in heaven, returning one day "on the clouds of heaven with power and great glory" (Matt. 24:30).

An interesting side note is that in Judea in Jesus' day, the Roman emperor had to formally recognize the right of a prince or king to rule. To acquire this authority, the prince or king had to travel to Rome. Archelaus, a son of Herod the Great, went to Rome to obtain a confirmation of the title his father had left him. Previously, his father had done the same thing to secure the aid of Mark Antony. Agrippa, the younger grandson of Herod the Great, also went to Rome to obtain the favor of Tiberius and to be confirmed in his government. So Jesus' listeners clearly understood the concept of traveling to a far country to receive authority to be king.

Details

The slaves are the followers of Christ who expect to be made princes, judges, and rulers at once if the kingdom comes in its fullness as Jesus enters Jerusalem. The apostles have dreamed of sitting next to Jesus in his kingdom, sharing his authority. But Jesus instead tells them they are slaves with much work to do. The number of slaves summoned—ten—does not appear to have any special significance, much as the number of virgins in the parable of the ten virgins does not reveal any profound truth other than that was the minimum number of people required to hold synagogue or have a wedding.

The Hebrew *maneh*, or Greek *mina*, translated "pound" in some versions, is a measure of weight equal to about 1.25 pounds. A marginal note in the New American Standard Bible says one mina is equal to about 100 days' wages. In any case, the nobleman tells his slaves to "engage in business" or put the money to work until he returns. "The pounds here denote the talents which God has given to his servants on earth to improve, and for which they must give an account in the day of judgment."[31]

The "subjects" symbolize the nation of Israel, and particularly the Jewish religious leaders, who have rejected Jesus as Messiah. They are fully aware that Archelaus had gone to Rome to obtain from Augustus a confirmation of his title to reign over the portion of Judea left to him by his father, Herod the Great. The Jews, opposing him, sent an embassy of fifty to Rome to ask Augustus to deny the title, but they failed. While Jesus is in no way of the same character as Archelaus, he is letting the Jewish leaders know that they have even less chance of successfully petitioning the heavenly Father against him than they had petitioning Augustus against Archelaus. Verse 27 may be seen as a dual prophecy in which Jesus foretells the destruction of Jerusalem and the Diaspora in 70 AD, as well as the final judgment of unbelievers before the great white throne (Rev. 20:11–15).

The rewards granted by the returning king should not necessarily be applied literally to the believer's reward at the judgment seat of Christ. Faithful believers may or may not be given cities to rule over. The point is that our reward in heaven will be in proportion to our faithfulness in improving our talents on earth.

The response of the third slave, who was entrusted with one mina, calls for a closer look. He wraps his mina in a cloth, or napkin, trying to convince his master that he has taken great care of it. Many gifted people guard their abilities but never employ them in the work of the kingdom and thus will be in a similar situation at the final judgment. Next, notice how the slave thought of his master—as someone to be feared, tough, and demanding. In fact, the word translated "tough" or "austere" is commonly applied to unripe fruit and means sour, unpleasant, or harsh. Further, his reference to his master as one who collects what he doesn't deposit (v. 21) is used to describe a man who finds what has been lost by another and keeps it himself. "All this is designed to show the sinner's view of God. He regards him as unjust, demanding more than man has *power* to render, and more, therefore, than God has a *right* to demand."[32]

31	*Barnes' Notes on the New Testament.*
32	*Barnes' Notes on the New Testament.*

The master tells the slave, "I will judge you by what you have said, you evil slave" (v. 22). Even though the master is neither unjust nor austere, the slave's supposing that he is should have spurred him to be obedient to the master's command. A sinner's mischaracterization of God does not excuse him or her of accountability on the day of reckoning.

Finally, the master orders that the mina be taken away from the unfaithful slave and given to the one who earned ten minas. Some are surprised at this and object, "Master, he has 10 minas" (v. 25). But the master's response illustrates a kingdom truth: to every person who is faithful and improves what God gives him or her, God will give that person more. As for the evil slave, it is interesting to note that he is not slaughtered with the rebelling subjects (v. 27). Perhaps instead Jesus is telling us what Paul writes about in 1 Corinthians 3:11–15, in which the believer who fails to build upon the foundation of Christ escapes the judgment, "yet it will be like an escape through fire."

Spiritual application

One day all believers will "stand before the judgment seat of Christ" (Rom. 14:10, KJV) and give an account of our stewardship. That judgment will not determine *where* we spend eternity, but *how*. We will have to give an answer for how we employed our time, talents, spiritual gifts, relationships, material possessions—all that Christ has entrusted to us while he has gone into heaven, preparing his return as King of Kings and Lord of Lords.

[Appendix]

HOW OTHERS DEFINE THE KINGDOM

We are defining the kingdom of heaven simply is God's reign—his authority to rule. Here's how others describe the kingdom:

☦ The Kingdom of God includes both His general sovereignty over the universe and His particular kingship over men who willfully acknowledge Him as King. Particularly, the Kingdom is the realm of salvation into which men enter by trustful, childlike commitment to Jesus Christ.

The Baptist Faith & Message

☦ The kingdom of God is the reign of God in the universe. It existed before the beginning of time, it is in operation today, and it will have a final consummation and perfection. It has application to both individuals (God's rule in the individual heart) and to the whole of society (God's rule at all levels).

Am I a Kingdom person? Empowering Kingdom Growth brochure

☦ The coming kingdom of God is nothing less than the subjection of all things to the rule and will of God ... When Christ has subjected all things to Himself and has destroyed sin and death, the kingdom of God in all its fullness will be manifest eternal and immortal on a renewed earth. This kingdom is the goal of redemption, the culmination of all previous revelations of God's kingdom. It is the rule of God the Father, God the Son incarnate as Messiah, and God the Holy Spirit over the earth with all its inhabitants and over the heavens and all contained therein forever.

Dr. Craig Blaising, executive vice president, provost and dean of the school of theology at Southwestern Baptist Theological Seminary; comments at "Communicating the Kingdom" conference, Ridgecrest, N.C., April 30, 2003

✠ The kingdom of God is the rule of God in the lives of believers and thus in the world.

Dr. James T. Draper, Jr., president, LifeWay Christian Resources, comments at "Communicating the Kingdom" conference, Ridgecrest, N.C., April 30, 2003

✠ Both in the Old Testament and in the New Testament the term "kingdom" is understood as dynamic in nature and refers primarily to the rule or reign of a king. It is seldom used in a static sense to refer to a territory. As a result, in the vast majority of instances it would be better to translate the expression "kingdom of God" as the "rule of God."

Baker's Evangelical Dictionary of Biblical Theology

✠ The kingdom of God is God's manifested reign in human affairs.

Henry Blackaby, *Experiencing God Holman Christian Standard Bible* notes

✠ God's kingly rule or sovereignty ... the rule of God ... the reign of God.

Holman Bible Dictionary

✠ The kingdom of God is the rule of God over the earth—particularly in the person of Jesus the Messiah.

Scofield Bible

✠ The key to an understanding of the kingdom of God is that the basic meaning of *basileia* is "rule," reign," or "dominion." Jesus proclaimed the kingdom of God as an event taking place in His own person and mission because He brought God's rule, reign, and dominion to earth.

No first-century Jew had any idea that the kingdom of God would come into history in the person of an ordinary man—a teacher who was meek and lowly. But Jesus demonstrated that the kingdom had come by healing the deaf, the blind, and lepers. He cast out demons and preached the Good News of the kingdom to the poor (Matt. 11:5).

Though Jesus brought the kingdom of God to earth, it will not be fully manifested until Jesus returns a second time. This is why Jesus taught us to pray: "Thy kingdom come on earth as it is in heaven" (Matt. 6:10). It is a prayer for God to manifest His reign so that His will be done on earth as it is in heaven. This will ultimately happen at Christ's second coming, but we can experience a foretaste of that kingdom here and now (Matt. 6:33). The kingdom of God in Jesus' person is like a hidden treasure or a pearl of great price, whose possession outranks all other goods (Matt. 13:44–46). We must seek it now, in anticipation of that one day, at the end of the age, when the kingdom of the world will become the dominion of our Lord and Jesus Christ (Rev. 11:15).

Holman Treasury of Key Bible Words

The Parable of the Sower

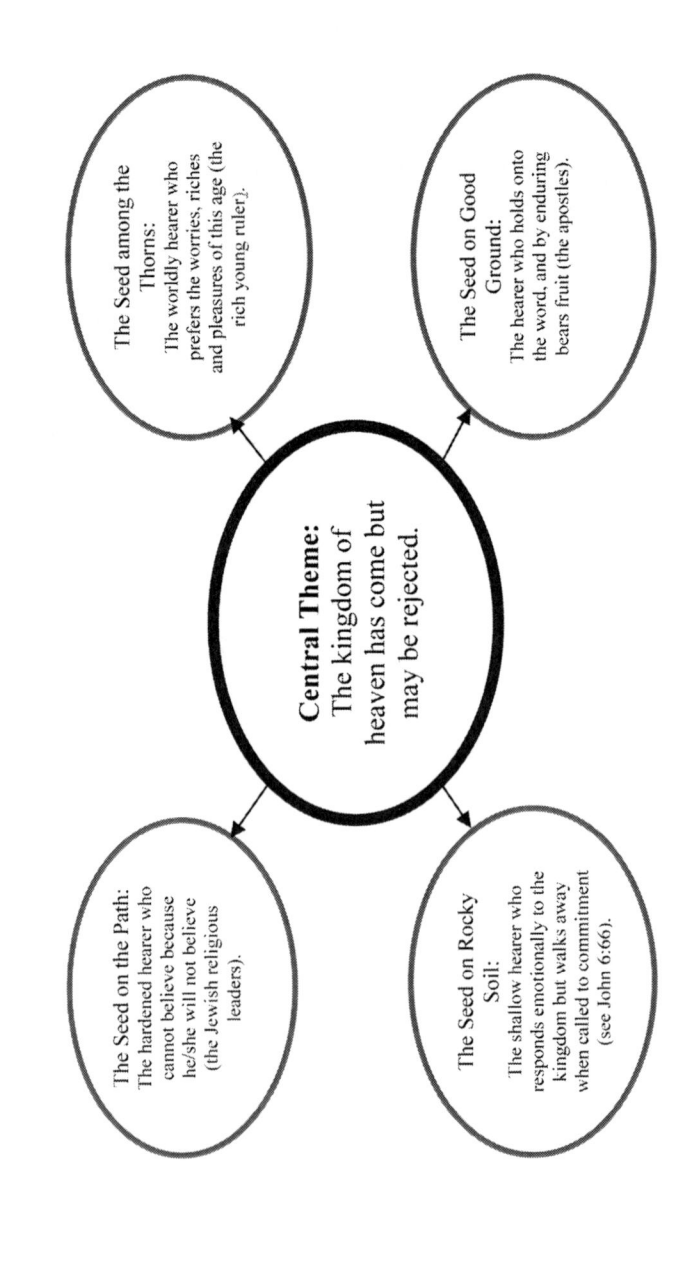

Central Theme: The kingdom of heaven has come but may be rejected.

- **The Seed on the Path:** The hardened hearer who cannot believe because he/she will not believe (the Jewish religious leaders).

- **The Seed on Rocky Soil:** The shallow hearer who responds emotionally to the kingdom but walks away when called to commitment (see John 6:66).

- **The Seed among the Thorns:** The worldly hearer who prefers the worries, riches and pleasures of this age (the rich young ruler).

- **The Seed on Good Ground:** The hearer who holds onto the word, and by enduring bears fruit (the apostles).

QUIZ

Test Your Knowledge of the Kingdom

Take this final exam

1. The kingdom of heaven is:
   a) Another name for the church
   b) The reign, or rule, of God
   c) A theme park in Orlando
   d) The nation of Israel during the millennium

2. True or false:
The kingdom of Satan operates totally outside the sovereignty of God.

3. True or false:
In Scripture, the kingdom of heaven and the kingdom of God are the same thing.

4. Jesus used parables to describe the kingdom of heaven because:
   a) They revealed the "mysteries" of the kingdom
   b) He fulfilled Old Testament prophecies that said the Messiah would speak in parables
   c) They were secret messages that later would be revealed in *The DaVinci Code*
   d) Both a) and b)
   e) I before E except after C

5. Concerning the kingdom of heaven, the Bible speaks of two great ages, which are:
   a) The stone age and the age of Aquarius
   b) 18 and 65
   c) The present evil age and the age to come
   d) The age of law and the age of grace

6. Which of the following are *not* parables of the kingdom of heaven:
   a) The sower, the storeroom, and the unmerciful servant
   b) The butcher, the baker, and the candlestick maker
   c) The ten virgins, the ten minas, and the wheat and tares

7. In the parable of the sheep and goats, who do the goats represent?
   a) Gentiles
   b) Unbelievers
   c) Carnal Christians
   d) Roman soldiers

8. Why does Jesus teach that some will be cast out of the kingdom?
   a) People may lose their salvation
   b) Some people will not earn the right to enter the kingdom and, if found there, will be asked to leave
   c) Some profess to know Jesus but are not really saved
   d) No one knows for sure if they're in or they're out

9. Who are the enemies of God that finally will be defeated when Jesus hands over the kingdom to his Father?
   a) False prophets, false preachers, and false teachers
   b) Pharisees, Sadducees, and scribes
   c) Bob and Carol, Ted and Alice
   d) Satan, sin, and death

10. When will the kingdom come in its fullness?
   a) When Christ returns and creates new heavens and a new earth
   b) It already has come, but secretly
   c) 2028
   d) When the Chicago Cubs win the World Series

11. Why did so many Jewish religious leaders fail to see Jesus as the promised Messiah?
   a) They thought he would be taller
   b) They were looking for a military and political Messiah
   c) Jesus did nothing to prove he was the Messiah
   d) They had no interest in a Messiah

12. The parable of the ten virgins teaches us:
   a) To be sexually pure
   b) To be ready for the return of Christ
   c) That Jewish weddings are a lot more fun than American weddings
   d) That the church will be asleep when Jesus returns

Answers: 1 – b; 2 – False; 3 – True; 4 – d; 5 – c; 6 – b; 7 – b; 8 – c; 9 – d; 10 – a; 11 – b; 12 – b.

The **Expectation** of the Kingdom

This Age → Messiah appears and ushers in the kingdom of heaven. → The Age to Come

The **Mystery** of the Kingdom

The Kingdom of Heaven
(present reality, future hope)

This Age → The Age to Come

Messiah appears as the suffering servant.

Messiah returns as the King of kings and Lord of lords.

Messiah casts Satan into hell; creates new heavens and earth.

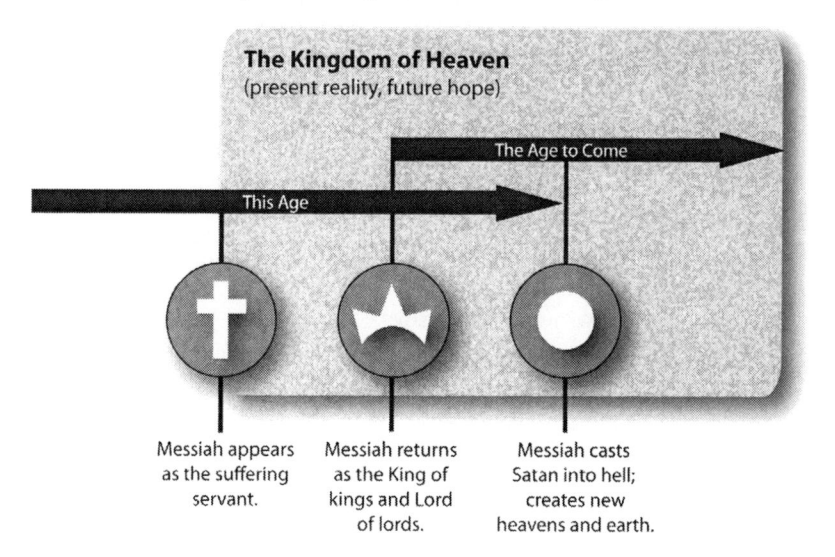

Illustration by Katie Shull

Present Reality

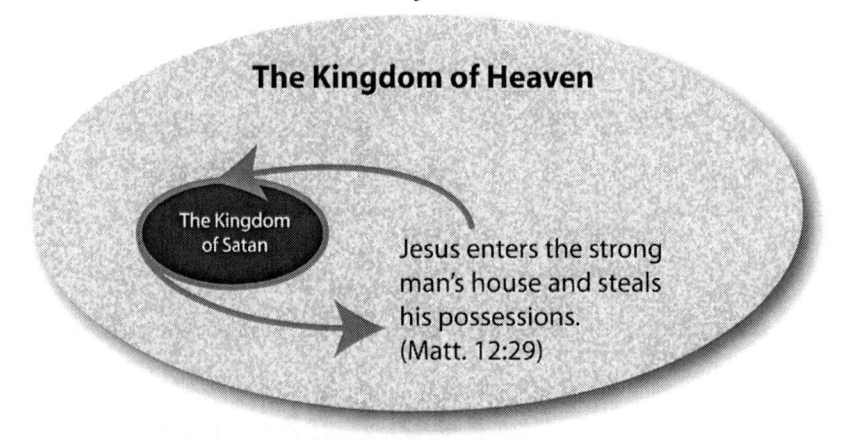

The Kingdom of Heaven

The Kingdom of Satan

Jesus enters the strong man's house and steals his possessions. (Matt. 12:29)

Future Hope

The Kingdom of Heaven

Jesus casts out Satan and destroys his kingdom. (Rev. 20:1-15)

The Kingdom of Satan destroyed

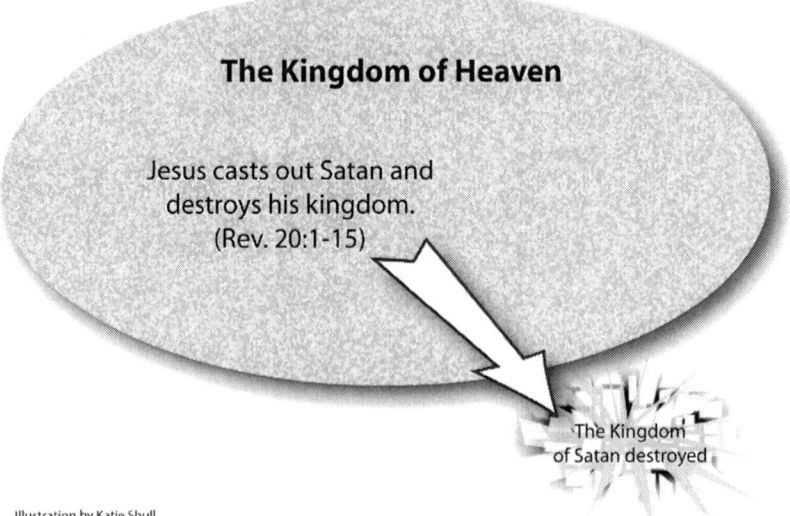

Illustration by Katie Shull

Kingdom Chart
The Once and Future Kingdom

The kingdom of heaven is:

God's reign	Now	Future
1 Chron. 29:11 - Yours, Lord, is the greatness and the power and the glory and the splendor and the majesty, for everything in the heavens and on earth belongs to You. Yours, Lord, is the kingdom, and You are exalted as head over all.	Matt. 3:2 - Repent, because the kingdom of heaven has come near!	Dan. 2:44 - In the days of those kings, the God of heaven will set up a kingdom that will never be destroyed, and this kingdom will not be left to another people. It will crush all these kingdoms and bring them to an end, but will itself endure forever.
Ps. 45:6 - Your throne, God, is forever and ever; the scepter of Your kingdom is a scepter of justice.	Matt 4:17 - From then on Jesus began to preach, "Repent, because the kingdom of heaven has come near!"	Dan. 7:14 - He was given authority to rule, and glory, and a kingdom; so that those of every people, nation, and language should serve Him. His dominion is an everlasting dominion that will not pass away, and His kingdom is one that will not be destroyed.
Ps. 103:19 - The Lord has established His throne in heaven, and His kingdom rules over all.	Matt. 4:23 - Jesus was going all over Galilee, teaching in their synagogues, preaching the good news of the kingdom, and healing every disease and sickness among the people.	Dan. 7:18 - But the holy ones of the Most High will receive the kingdom and possess it forever, yes, forever and ever.

God's reign	Now	Future
Ps. 145:13 - Your kingdom is an everlasting kingdom; Your rule is for all generations.	Matt 5:3 - Blessed are the poor in spirit, because the kingdom of heaven is theirs.	Dan. 7:22 - until the Ancient of Days arrived and a judgment was given in favor of the holy ones of the Most High, for the time had come, and the holy ones took possession of the kingdom.
Dan. 4:3 - How great are His miracles, and how mighty His wonders! His kingdom is an eternal kingdom, and His dominion is from generation to generation.	Matt 5:10 - Blessed are those who are persecuted for righteousness, because the kingdom of heaven is theirs.	Dan. 7:27 - The kingdom, dominion, and greatness of the kingdoms under all of heaven will be given to the people, the holy ones of the Most High. His kingdom will be an everlasting kingdom, and all rulers will serve and obey Him.
Dan. 6:26 - I issue a decree that in all my royal dominion, people must tremble in fear before the God of Daniel: For He is the living God, and He endures forever; His kingdom will never be destroyed, and His dominion has no end.	Matt 5:19 - Therefore, whoever breaks one of the least of these commandments and teaches people to do so will be called least in the kingdom of heaven. But whoever practices and teaches [these commandments] will be called great in the kingdom of heaven.	Matt. 6:10 - Your kingdom come. Your will be done on earth as it is in heaven.

God's reign	Now	Future
Matt. 6:13 - And do not bring us into temptation, but deliver us from the evil one. [For Yours is the kingdom and the power and the glory forever. Amen.]	Matt. 5:20 - For I tell you, unless your righteousness surpasses that of the scribes and Pharisees, you will never enter the kingdom of heaven.	Matt. 7:21 - Not everyone who says to Me, 'Lord, Lord!' will enter the kingdom of heaven, but [only]the one who does the will of My Father in heaven.
Matt. 16:19 - I will give you the keys of the kingdom of heaven, and whatever you bind on earth is already bound in heaven, and whatever you loose on earth is already loosed in heaven.	Matt. 6:33 - But seek first the kingdom of God and His righteousness, and all these things will be provided for you.	Matt. 8:11 - I tell you that many will come from east and west, and recline at the table with Abraham, Isaac, and Jacob in the kingdom of heaven.
Mark 11:10 - Blessed is the coming kingdom of our father David! Hosanna in the highest heaven! (Jews rejoicing at Jesus' triumphant entry into Jerusalem because they saw God's reign through Israel being restored.)	Matt. 9:35 - Then Jesus went to all the towns and villages, teaching in their synagogues, preaching the good news of the kingdom, and healing every disease and every sickness.	Matt. 8:12 - But the sons of the kingdom will be thrown into the outer darkness. In that place there will be weeping and gnashing of teeth.
Luke 1:33 - He will reign over the house of Jacob forever, and His kingdom will have no end.	Matt. 10:7 - As you go, announce this: 'The kingdom of heaven has come near.'	Matt. 13:41 - The Son of Man will send out His angels, and they will gather from His kingdom everything that causes sin and those guilty of lawlessness.

God's reign	Now	Future
John 18:36 - "My kingdom is not of this world," said Jesus. "If My kingdom were of this world, My servants would fight, so that I wouldn't be handed over to the Jews. As it is, My kingdom does not have its origin here."	Matt. 11:11 - I assure you: Among those born of women no one greater than John the Baptist has appeared, but the least in the kingdom of heaven is greater than he.	Matt. 13:43 - Then the righteous will shine like the sun in their Father's kingdom. Anyone who has ears should listen!
Acts 1:3 - After He had suffered, He also presented Himself alive to them by many convincing proofs, appearing to them during 40 days and speaking about the kingdom of God.	Matt. 11:12 - From the days of John the Baptist until now, the kingdom of heaven has been suffering violence, and the violent have been seizing it by force.	Matt. 13:47 - Again, the kingdom of heaven is like a large net thrown into the sea. It collected every kind [of fish] …
Acts 1:6 - So when they had come together, they asked Him, "Lord, at this time are You restoring the kingdom to Israel?"	Matt. 12:28 - If I drive out demons by the Spirit of God, then the kingdom of God has come to you.	Matt. 16:28 - I assure you: There are some standing here who will not taste death until they see the Son of Man coming in His kingdom.
Rom. 14:16-17 - Therefore, do not let your good be slandered, for the kingdom of God is not eating and drinking, but righteousness, peace, and joy in the Holy Spirit.	Matt. 13:11 - He answered them, "Because the secrets of the kingdom of heaven have been given for you to know, but it has not been given to them."	Matt. 20:21 - "What do you want?" He asked her. "Promise," she said to Him, "that these two sons of mine may sit, one on Your right and the other on Your left, in Your kingdom."

God's reign	**Now**	**Future**
1 Cor. 4:20 - For the kingdom of God is not in talk but in power.	Matt. 13:19 - When anyone hears the word about the kingdom and doesn't understand it, the evil one comes and snatches away what was sown in his heart. This is the one sown along the path.	Matt. 21:43 - Therefore I tell you, the kingdom of God will be taken away from you and given to a nation producing its fruit (foretelling national judgment of Israel, which came in 70 A.D.).
Heb. 1:8 - ... but about the Son: Your throne, O God, is forever and ever, and the scepter of Your kingdom is a scepter of justice.	Matt. 13:24 - He presented another parable to them: "The kingdom of heaven may be compared to a man who sowed good seed in his field."	Matt. 25:1 - Then the kingdom of heaven will be like 10 virgins who took their lamps and went out to meet the groom.
	Matt. 13:31 - He presented another parable to them: "The kingdom of heaven is like a mustard seed that a man took and sowed in his field."	Matt. 25:14 - For it is just like a man going on a journey. He called his own slaves and turned over his possessions to them (also a present reference).
	Matt 13:33 - He told them another parable: "The kingdom of heaven is like yeast that a woman took and mixed into 50 pounds of flour until it spread through all of it."	Matt. 25:34 - Then the King will say to those on His right, 'Come, you who are blessed by My Father, inherit the kingdom prepared for you from the foundation of the world.'

God's reign	**Now**	**Future**
	Matt. 13:38 - the field is the world; and the good seed—these are the sons of the kingdom. The weeds are the sons of the evil one …	Matt. 26:29 - But I tell you, from this moment I will not drink of this fruit of the vine until that day when I drink it in a new way in My Father's kingdom with you.
	Matt. 13:44 - The kingdom of heaven is like treasure, buried in a field, that a man found and reburied. Then in his joy he goes and sells everything he has and buys that field.	Mark 9:1 - Then He said to them, " I assure you: There are some standing here who will not taste death until they see the kingdom of God come in power."
	Matt. 13:45-6 - Again, the kingdom of heaven is like a merchant in search of fine pearls. When he found one priceless pearl, he went and sold everything he had, and bought it.	Mark 14:25 - I assure you: I will no longer drink of the fruit of the vine until that day when I drink it in a new way in the kingdom of God.
	Matt. 13:52 - "Therefore," He said to them, "every student of Scripture instructed in the kingdom of heaven is like a landowner who brings out of his storeroom what is new and what is old."	Mark 15:43 - Joseph of Arimathea, a prominent member of the Sanhedrin who was himself looking forward to the kingdom of God, came and boldly went in to Pilate and asked for Jesus' body.

God's reign	**Now**	**Future**
	Matt. 18:1 - At that time the disciples came to Jesus and said, "Who is greatest in the kingdom of heaven?"	Luke 9:27 - I tell you the truth: there are some standing here who will not taste death until they see the kingdom of God.
	Matt. 18:3-4 - "I assure you," He said, "unless you are converted and become like children, you will never enter the kingdom of heaven. Therefore, whoever humbles himself like this child—this one is the greatest in the kingdom of heaven."	Luke 11:2 - He said to them, "Whenever you pray, say: Father, Your name be honored as holy. Your kingdom come."
	Matt. 18:23 - For this reason, the kingdom of heaven can be compared to a king who wanted to settle accounts with his slaves.	Luke 13:28-29 - There will be weeping and gnashing of teeth in that place, when you see Abraham, Isaac, Jacob, and all the prophets in the kingdom of God but yourselves thrown out. They will come from east and west, from north and south, and recline at the table in the kingdom of God.

God's reign	Now	Future
	Matt. 19:12 - For there are eunuchs who were born that way from their mother's womb, there are eunuchs who were made by men, and there are eunuchs who have made themselves that way because of the kingdom of heaven. Let anyone accept this who can.	Luke 14:15 - When one of those who reclined at the table with Him heard these things, he said to Him, "The one who will eat bread in the kingdom of God is blessed!"
	Matt. 19:14 - Then Jesus said, "Leave the children alone, and don't try to keep them from coming to Me, because the kingdom of heaven is made up of people like this."	Luke 19:11-12, 15 - As they were listening to this, He went on to tell a parable because He was near Jerusalem, and they thought the kingdom of God was going to appear right away. Therefore He said: "A nobleman traveled to a far country to receive for himself authority to be king and then return.... At his return, having received the authority to be king, he summoned those slaves he had given the money to so he could find out how much they had made in business" (also a present reference).

God's reign	**Now**	**Future**
	Matt. 19:23-24 - Then Jesus said to His disciples, "I assure you: It will be hard for a rich person to enter the kingdom of heaven! Again I tell you, it is easier for a camel to go through the eye of a needle than for a rich person to enter the kingdom of God."	Luke 21:31 - In the same way, when you see these things happening, recognize that the kingdom of God is near.
	Matt. 20:1 - For the kingdom of heaven is like a landowner who went out early in the morning to hire workers for his vineyard.	Luke 22:16, 18 - For I tell you, I will not eat it again until it is fulfilled in the kingdom of God.... For I tell you, from now on I will not drink of the fruit of the vine until the kingdom of God comes.
	Matt. 21:31 - "Which of the two did his father's will?" "The first," they said. Jesus said to them, "I assure you: Tax collectors and prostitutes are entering the kingdom of God before you!"	Luke 22:29-30 - I bestow on you a kingdom, just as My Father bestowed one on Me, so that you may eat and drink at My table in My kingdom. And you will sit on thrones judging the 12 tribes of Israel.
	Matt. 22:2 - The kingdom of heaven may be compared to a king who gave a wedding banquet for his son.	Luke 23:42 - Then he said, "Jesus, remember me when You come into Your kingdom!"

God's reign	**Now**	**Future**
	Matt. 23:13 - But woe to you, scribes and Pharisees, hypocrites! You lock up the kingdom of heaven from people. For you don't go in, and you don't allow those entering to go in.	Luke 23:50-51 - There was a good and righteous man named Joseph, a member of the Sanhedrin, who had not agreed with their plan and action. He was from Arimathea, a Judean town, and was looking forward to the kingdom of God.
	Matt. 24:14 - This good news of the kingdom will be proclaimed in all the world as a testimony to all nations. And then the end will come.	1 Cor. 6:9-10 - Do you not know that the unjust will not inherit God's kingdom? Do not be deceived: no sexually immoral people, idolaters, adulterers, male prostitutes, homosexuals, thieves, greedy people, drunkards, revilers, or swindlers will inherit God's kingdom.
	Matt. 25:14 - For it is just like a man going on a journey. He called his own slaves and turned over his possessions to them (also a future reference).	1 Cor. 15:24 - Then comes the end, when He hands over the kingdom to God the Father, when He abolishes all rule and all authority and power.

God's reign	**Now**	**Future**
	Mark 1:14-15 - After John was arrested, Jesus went to Galilee, preaching the good news of God: "The time is fulfilled, and the kingdom of God has come near. Repent and believe in the good news!"	1 Cor. 15:50 - Brothers, I tell you this: flesh and blood cannot inherit the kingdom of God, and corruption cannot inherit incorruption.
	Mark 3:24 - If a kingdom is divided against itself, that kingdom cannot stand (reference to Satan's kingdom and the kingdom of God's invasion of it).	Gal. 5:19-21 - Now the works of the flesh are obvious: sexual immorality, moral impurity, promiscuity, idolatry, sorcery, hatreds, strife, jealousy, outbursts of anger, selfish ambitions, dissensions, factions, envy, drunkenness, carousing, and anything similar, about which I tell you in advance—as I told you before—that those who practice such things will not inherit the kingdom of God.
	Mark 4:11 - He answered them, "The secret of the kingdom of God has been granted to you, but to those outside, everything comes in parables …"	Eph. 5:5 - For know and recognize this: no sexually immoral or impure or greedy person, who is an idolater, has an inheritance in the kingdom of the Messiah and of God.

God's reign	**Now**	**Future**
	Mark 4:26 - "The kingdom of God is like this," He said. "A man scatters seed on the ground …"	2 Thess. 1:5 - It is a clear evidence of God's righteous judgment that you will be counted worthy of God's kingdom, for which you also are suffering …
	Mark 4:30 - And He said: "How can we illustrate the kingdom of God, or what parable can we use to describe it?"	2 Tim. 4:1 - Before God and Christ Jesus, who is going to judge the living and the dead, and by His appearing and His kingdom, I solemnly charge you …
	Mark 9:47 - And if your eye causes your downfall, gouge it out. It is better for you to enter the kingdom of God with one eye than to have two eyes and be thrown into hell …	2 Tim. 4:18 - The Lord will rescue me from every evil work and will bring me safely into His heavenly kingdom. To Him be the glory forever and ever! Amen.
	Mark 10:14-15 - When Jesus saw it, He was indignant and said to them, "Let the little children come to Me. Don't stop them, for the kingdom of God belongs to such as these. I assure you: Whoever does not welcome the kingdom of God like a little child will never enter it."	James 2:5 - Listen, my dear brothers: Didn't God choose the poor in this world to be rich in faith and heirs of the kingdom that He has promised to those who love Him?

God's reign	**Now**	**Future**
	Mark 10:23-25 - Jesus looked around and said to His disciples, "How hard it is for those who have wealth to enter the kingdom of God!" But the disciples were astonished at His words. Again Jesus said to them, "Children, how hard it is to enter the kingdom of God! It is easier for a camel to go through the eye of a needle than for a rich person to enter the kingdom of God."	2 Peter 1:11 - For in this way, entry into the eternal kingdom of our Lord and Savior Jesus Christ will be richly supplied to you.
	Mark 12:34 - When Jesus saw that he answered intelligently, He said to him, "You are not far from the kingdom of God." And no one dared to question Him any longer.	Rev. 12:10 - Then I heard a loud voice in heaven say: The salvation and the power and the kingdom of our God and the authority of His Messiah have now come, because the accuser of our brothers has been thrown out: the one who accuses them before our God day and night.
	Luke 4:43 - But He said to them, "I must proclaim the good news about the kingdom of God to the other towns also, because I was sent for this purpose."	

God's reign	Now	Future
	Luke 6:20 - Then looking up at His disciples, He said: "Blessed are you who are poor, because the kingdom of God is yours."	
	Luke 7:28 – I tell you, among those born of women no one is greater than John, but the least in the kingdom of God is greater than he.	
	Luke 8:1 - Soon afterwards He was traveling from one town and village to another, preaching and telling the good news of the kingdom of God. The Twelve were with Him …	
	Luke 8:10 - So He said, "The secrets of the kingdom of God have been given for you to know, but to the rest it is in parables, so that Looking they may not see, and hearing they may not understand."	
	Luke 9:2 - Then He sent them to proclaim the kingdom of God and to heal the sick.	

God's reign	Now	Future
	Luke 9:11 - When the crowds found out, they followed Him. He welcomed them, spoke to them about the kingdom of God, and cured those who needed healing.	
	Luke 9:60 - But He told him, "Let the dead bury their own dead, but you go and spread the news of the kingdom of God."	
	Luke 9:62 - But Jesus said to him, "No one who puts his hand to the plow and looks back is fit for the kingdom of God."	
	Luke 10:9 - Heal the sick who are there, and tell them, 'The kingdom of God has come near you.'	
	Luke 10:11 - 'We are wiping off [as a witness] against you even the dust of your town that clings to our feet. Know this for certain: the kingdom of God has come near.'	
	Luke 11:20 - If I drive out demons by the finger of God, then the kingdom of God has come to you.	

God's reign	Now	Future
	Luke 12:31-32 - But seek His kingdom, and these things will be provided for you. Don't be afraid, little flock, because your Father delights to give you the kingdom.	
	Luke 13:18-19 - He said therefore, "What is the kingdom of God like, and what can I compare it to? It's like a mustard seed that a man took and sowed in his garden. It grew and became a tree, and the birds of the sky nested in its branches."	
	Luke 13:20-21 - Again He said, "What can I compare the kingdom of God to? It's like yeast that a woman took and mixed into 50 pounds of flour until it spread through the entire mixture."	
	Luke 16:16 - The Law and the Prophets were until John; since then, the good news of the kingdom of God has been proclaimed, and everyone is strongly urged to enter it.	

God's reign	Now	Future
	Luke 17:20-21 - Being asked by the Pharisees when the kingdom of God will come, He answered them, "The kingdom of God is not coming with something observable; no one will say, 'Look here!' or 'There!' For you see, the kingdom of God is among you."	
	Luke 18:16-17 - Jesus, however, invited them: "Let the little children come to Me, and don't stop them, because the kingdom of God belongs to such as these. I assure you: Whoever does not welcome the kingdom of God like a little child will never enter it."	
	Luke 18:24-25 - Seeing that he became sad, Jesus said, "How hard it is for those who have wealth to enter the kingdom of God! For it is easier for a camel to go through the eye of a needle than for a rich person to enter the kingdom of God."	

God's reign	Now	Future
	Luke 18:29-30 - So He said to them, "I assure you: There is no one who has left a house, wife or brothers, parents or children because of the kingdom of God, who will not receive many times more at this time, and eternal life in the age to come."	
	Luke 19:11-12, 15 - As they were listening to this, He went on to tell a parable because He was near Jerusalem, and they thought the kingdom of God was going to appear right away. Therefore He said: "A nobleman traveled to a far country to receive for himself authority to be king and then return.... At his return, having received the authority to be king, he summoned those slaves he had given the money to so he could find out how much they had made in business" (also a future reference).	
	John 3:3 - Jesus replied, "I assure you: Unless someone is born again, he cannot see the kingdom of God."	

God's Reign	**Now**	**Future**
	John 3:5 - Jesus answered, "I assure you: Unless someone is born of water and the Spirit, he cannot enter the kingdom of God."	
	Acts 8:12 - But when they believed Philip, as he proclaimed the good news about the kingdom of God and the name of Jesus Christ, both men and women were baptized.	
	Acts 14:21-22 - After they had evangelized that town and made many disciples, they returned to Lystra, to Iconium, and to Antioch, strengthening the hearts of the disciples by encouraging them to continue in the faith, and by telling them, "It is necessary to pass through many troubles on our way into the kingdom of God."	
	Acts 19:8 - Then he entered the synagogue and spoke boldly over a period of three months, engaging in discussion and trying to persuade them about the things related to the kingdom of God.	
	Acts 20:25 - And now I know that none of you, among whom I went about preaching the kingdom, will ever see my face again.	

God's reign	**Now**	**Future**
	Acts 28:23 - After arranging a day with him, many came to him at his lodging. From dawn to dusk he expounded and witnessed about the kingdom of God. He persuaded them concerning Jesus from both the Law of Moses and the Prophets.	
	Acts 28:30-31 - Then he stayed two whole years in his own rented house. And he welcomed all who visited him, proclaiming the kingdom of God and teaching the things concerning the Lord Jesus Christ with full boldness and without hindrance.	
	Col. 1:13 - He has rescued us from the domain of darkness and transferred us into the kingdom of the Son He loves …	
	Col. 4:11 - … and so does Jesus who is called Justus. These alone of the circumcision are my co-workers for the kingdom of God, and they have been a comfort to me.	

God's reign	Now	Future
	1 Thess. 2:12 - ... we encouraged, comforted, and implored each one of you to walk worthy of God, who calls you into His own kingdom and glory. Heb. 12:28 - Therefore, since we are receiving a kingdom that cannot be shaken, let us hold on to grace. By it, we may serve God acceptably, with reverence and awe ... Rev. 1:9 - I, John, your brother and partner in the tribulation, kingdom, and perseverance in Jesus, was on the island called Patmos because of God's word and the testimony about Jesus.	

About the Author

Rob Phillips is a certified apologetics instructor with more than twenty years of experience in preaching, teaching, and training Christians to "contend for the faith that was delivered to the saints once for all" (Jude 3).

He serves as an adult Bible study leader at Brentwood (Tennessee) Baptist Church and works with the North American Mission Board and the Tennessee Baptist Convention to speak in churches and lead training events in apologetics. In 2008 he launched Oncedelivered.net, an apologetics Web site that features free downloadable resources. The site also provides information on how to contact Phillips to schedule training events and speaking opportunities.

Phillips worked more than twenty years in public and media relations for Phillips Petroleum Company and Wal-Mart Stores, Inc., while at the same time serving as associate pastor of Bartlesville (Oklahoma) Southern Baptist Church and speaking in churches throughout the Southwest. He currently works full time as director of communications for LifeWay Christian Resources in Nashville, Tennessee.

Short-term mission projects have taken him to Honduras, Nicaragua, Cuba, Brazil, Chile, and the Philippines.

A graduate of Oklahoma Baptist University, Phillips and his wife Nancy have two grown children.